OSPREY COMBAT AIRCRAFT • 4

MOSQUITO
BOMBER/FIGHTER-BOMBER UNITS OF WORLD WAR 2

SERIES EDITOR: TONY HOLMES

OSPREY COMBAT AIRCRAFT • 4

MOSQUITO
BOMBER/FIGHTER-BOMBER UNITS OF WORLD WAR 2

Martin Bowman

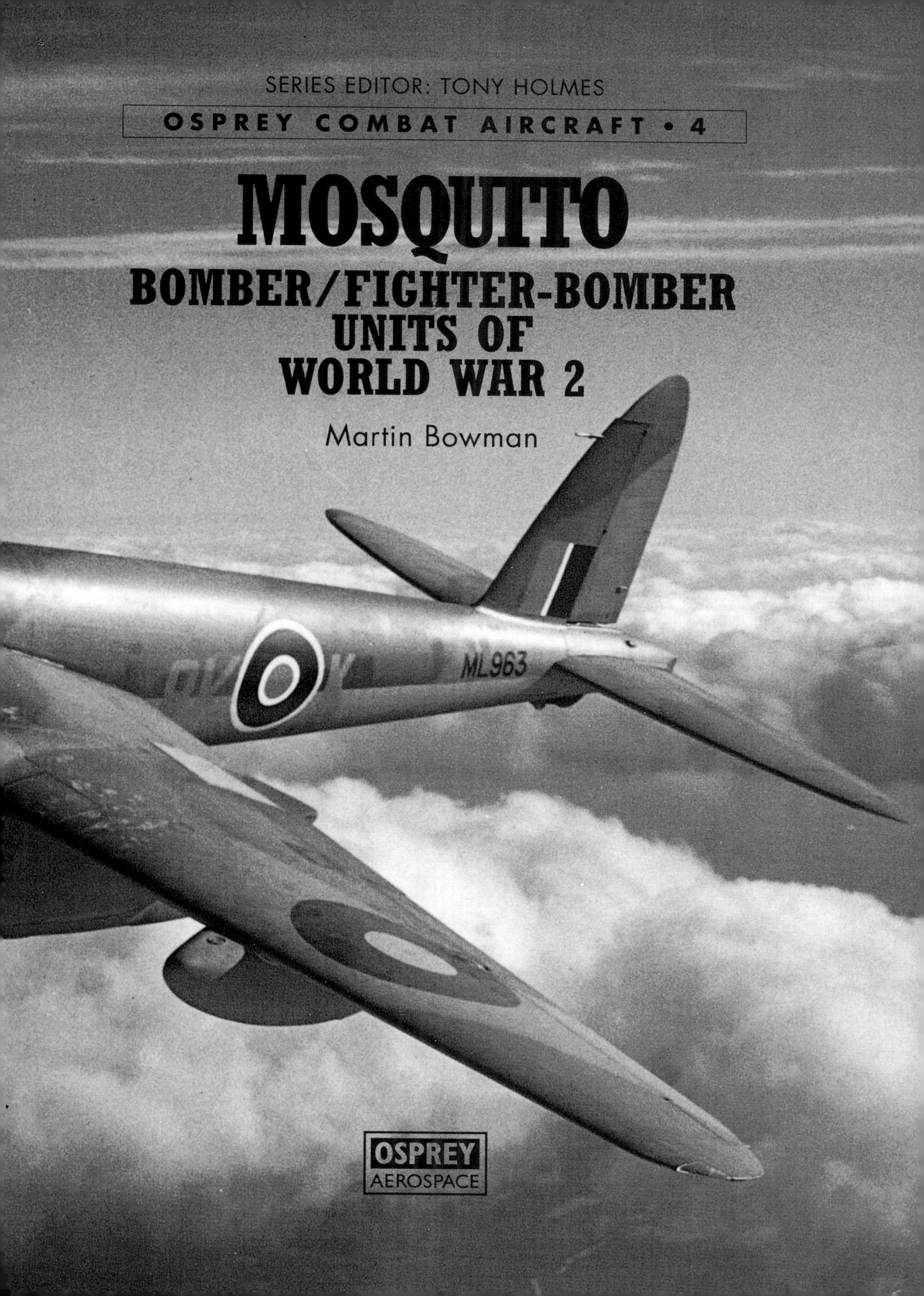

ML963

OSPREY
AEROSPACE

Front cover

On 11 April 1944 six Mosquito FB VIs of No 613 'City of Manchester' Sqn performed one of the most accurate low-level bombing raids of the war against the Dutch Central Population Registry, housed in the Kunstzaal Kleizkamp Art Gallery close to the Peace Palace. The registry had become a prime target following its use by the Gestapo to hold records pertaining to Dutch families deemed suitable for deportation to concentration camps, or for reprisal executions of the relatives of resistance fighters. The following description of the raid was printed in Leslie Hunt's volume *Twenty-One Squadrons* (Garnstone Press, 1972);

'On 11th April, flying at only 50 ft, Wg Cdr Bateson led six Mosquitos, the plan being for three pairs to come in at two-minute intervals dropping high-explosives and incendiary bombs. Bateson led the first pair in, skimming house tops, making straight for the target building. A German sentry on duty at the front door screamed with horror as he threw away his rifle and ran for his life. Flt Lt P C Cobley, in the second plane, saw his leader's bombs going "right in the front door". A parade was in progress in the yard behind the building and some off-duty soldiers were playing football. No further goals were scored as Cobley's aircraft scattered troops in all directions with more bombs, right on target. Sqn Ldr Newman led in the next pair. The house was now partly obscured by smoke but he and his colleague dropped incendiaries across it. Last in were Flt Lt V A Hester and a Dutch pilot. Hester attacked with incendiaries and delayed-action high-explosives but the Dutchman's bombs hung up. Despite two more circuits and runs over the target he could not release them and had to return home without scoring a hit.'

Having reduced the five-storey building to rubble without causing any damage to surrounding structures, the Mosquitos returned to Swanton Morley, in Norfolk. A first-hand account of the raid, entitled 'The House in the Hague', was given by Wg Cdr Bateson on BBC radio on 1 May 1944, and three days later participating crews were presented to His Majesty King George VI (cover artwork by Iain Wyllie)

First published in Great Britain in 1997 by Osprey Publishing, Elms Court, Chapel Way, Botley, Oxford, OX2 9LP

Reprinted Autumn 1998

ISBN 1 85532 690 6

Edited by Tony Holmes
Page design by TT Designs, T & S Truscott
Cover Artwork by Iain Wyllie
Aircraft Profiles by Chris Davey
Figure Artwork by Mike Chappell
Scale Drawings by Arthur Bentley

Printed in Hong Kong

ACKNOWLEDGEMENTS

The author would like to thank the following individuals for their valued assistance during the compilation of this volume: Sqn Ldr John Archbold, RAF Retd; Eric Atkins DFC*, KW*, RAF Retd, Chairman of the Mosquito Aircrew Association; BAe; Mike Bailey; Philip Beck; Andy Bird; Sqn Ldr Ed Boulter; Les Bulmer, RAF Retd; Sqn Ldr Ed Bulpett, CRO at RAF Marham; Philip Birtles; Derek Carter; Tom Cushing; Ern Dunkley, RAAF Retd; E S Gates; Grp Capt J R 'Benny' Goodman DFC*, AFC, AE; Ken Greenwood; T M 'Mac' Hetherington, RCAF Retd; Philip Jarrett; R E 'Bob' Kirkpatrick, RAF Retd; Ron Smith; Vic Hester, RAF Retd; G A B Lord, RAF Retd; P D Morris; Ron Mackay; A P 'Pat' O'Hara DFM, RAF Retd; Wg Cdr George Parry DSO, DFC*; Sqn Ldr Charles Patterson DSO, DFC, RAF Retd; Alf Pridmore; RAAF Museum Point Cook; Harry Randall-Cutler, RAF Retd; Alan Sanderson; RAF Swanton Morley; Jerry Scutts; Jim Shortland; Knowle Shrimpton DFC, RAAF Retd; Ken Hyde, archivist for the Shuttleworth Collection; Graham M Simons; Andy Thomas; Geoff Thomas; Ben Walsh; and the late J Ralph Wood DFC, CDR, CAF Retd.

EDITOR'S NOTE

To make this new series as authoritative as possible, the editor would be interested in hearing from any individual who may have relevant photographs, documentation or first-hand experiences relating to combat aircraft, and their crews, of the various theatres of war. Any material used will be fully credited to its original source. Please write to Tony Holmes at 1 Bradbourne Road, Sevenoaks, Kent, TN13 3PZ, Great Britain.

CONTENTS

LOW-LEVEL RAIDERS

In November 1941, Blenheim-equipped No 105 Sqn of No 2 Group at Swanton Morley airfield, in Norfolk, became the first unit in RAF Bomber Command to finally receive the revolutionary new de Havilland B Mk IV Mosquito. Although the bomber/photo-reconnaissance (PR) prototype (W4050) had flown on 25 November 1940, the only versions in service by 1941 were those used for PR work. Production had only begun at all after a long, and sometimes painful, development phase, and at one stage the project had almost been abandoned altogether. At Hatfield, de Havilland management knew that their two-crew, unarmed, wooden bomber design, which relied on speed alone to out-distance enemy fighters, was a winner, even before it had left the drawing board. However, in London at this time unarmed bombers were an anathema. When de Havilland finally received a contract for 150 Mosquitoes on 30 December 1940 it was not specified how many would be fighters and how many would be photo-reconnaissance versions, let alone bombers.

In June 1941 the fighter version was approved. Convincing the Air Ministry that they should also order into production an unarmed, wooden, bomber version was only achieved the following month after

On 15 November 1941 de Havilland Chief Test Pilot, Geoffrey de Havilland Jr, demonstrated prototype Mosquito W4064 to Wg Cdr Peter H A Simmons DFC, OC No 105 Sqn, and his air- and groundcrews at their Swanton Morley base. That same month the first Mk IVs came off the Hatfield production lines, and on 17 November W4066 became the premier Mosquito B Mk IV bomber to enter RAF service when it was received by Simmons' unit – No 105 Sqn's first operation took place on 31 May 1942. B Mk IVs were initially so scarce that No 105 Sqn often had to share aircraft with its sister-squadron, No 139, in order to perform operations from its Norfolk base (*RAF Marham*)

Aircrews from both Nos 105 and 139 Sqns pose beside a B Mk IV at RAF Marham. At far left (with his back to the camera) is Jamaican-born Flg Off Pereira of No 139 Sqn, seen here talking to Flt Lt J Gordon (unfastening his 'Mae West'). No 139 Sqn flew their first operation on 2 July 1942 when two B Mk IVs carried out a high level bombing raid on Flensburg (*RAF Marham*)

strong lobbying by de Havilland, but especially when the Mosquito was seen to perform exactly as the company said it would. In trials in December 1940, the prototype, which was fitted with Merlin 21 engines with two-speed, single-stage, superchargers, had reached speeds of 255 mph. On 16 January 1941 W4050 outpaced a Spitfire in tests at 6000 ft, and in July the aircraft (this time fitted with Merlin 61s) reached 433 mph at 28,500 ft!

When the Air Ministry finally gave the go ahead for the bomber variant, it ordered some 50 aircraft, each capable of carrying four 250-lb bombs, and further specified that the last 10 aircraft out of the 19 PR Mosquitoes contracted should also be completed as unarmed bombers. These aircraft retained the short nacelles of the early models, and came to be known as the B IV Series I. W4072, the prototype B IV bomber, flew for the first time on 8 September 1941. The 292 B IV Series II bombers that followed (27 were later converted into PR Mk IVs) differed in having longer nacelles, and they could also carry two 50-gallon droppable wing tanks in addition to a 2000-lb bomb load – made possible by simply shortening the tail stabiliser of each bomb.

On 15 November 1941 No 105 Sqn's OC, Wg Cdr P H A Simmons DFC, and his crews were greatly impressed when de Havilland Chief Test Pilot, Geoffrey de Havilland Jr, arrived over the airfield in W4064. The 'wooden wonder' was far removed from the Blenheim both in power and performance, and Geoffrey de Havilland treated the unit to a spectacular piece of flying, racing low across the grass airfield at 500 ft at a speed in the region of 300 mph. The Hatfield test pilot then put the Mosquito into a vertical bank at about 3000 ft, before pulling into a tight circle that produced vapour trails from the wing tips. Only the air gunners failed to be impressed, as they were now surplus to requirements on the Mosquito, while the navigators would have to learn to operate the radio.

On 17 November W4066 – the first Mosquito bomber to enter RAF service – was received at Swanton Morley by the AOC No 2 Group, AVM d'Albiac, and his staff. A further three Mk IVs (W4064, W4068 and W4071) were later delivered by Geoffrey de Havilland and Pat Fillingham. In December No 105 Sqn moved to Horsham St Faith, just outside Norwich. Deliveries of the new aircraft were slow because of the need to develop the shortened-vane 500-lb bomb, which would then allow the Mosquito to carry four 500 'pounders' in place of the smaller 250-lb bombs. By mid-May 1942 just eight Mk.IVs were operational, one of which was fitted with Lorenz beam approach equipment, while another (DK286) boasted the new Mk XIV bomb sight for operational testing.

No 2 Group were eager to despatch Mosquitoes on operations as soon as possible, and the de Havilland bomber duly made its combat debut at dawn on 31 May 1942 in the wake of the RAF's first ever 'Thousand Bomber' raid – the latter had attacked Cologne. Four Mk IVs (the first of which was piloted by Sqn Ldr A R Oakeshott DFC), armed with 500-lb bombs and F.24 cameras, took off from St Faith and dropped their ordnance on the recently devastated city. They then quickly photographed the results of Operation *Millenium* before returning to base. Oakeshott was the first to reach the target area, overflying Cologne at 24,000 ft and dropping his four bombs from this height. However, smoke from the 'Thousand Bomber' raid had by this time settled at 14,000 ft, thus obstructing the squadron leader's his photo run. Oakeshott duly returned to Norfolk, but two other Mosquitoes (flown by Plt Offs W D Kennard and E R Johnson) were downed by anti-aircraft fire over the target area.

Just after noon on the following day two crews (Plt Off Costello-Bowen and Wt Off Tommy Broom, and Flt Lt J E Houlston and Flt Sgt J L Armitage) again bombed Cologne from high level, although on this occasion they both returned safely. Later that afternoon Sqn Ldr R J Channer DFC took off and flew in thick cloud to within 60 miles of the city before diving down at almost 380 mph to low level to take more photographs. On the evening of 1 June two more Mosquito B Mk IVs sortied to Cologne but one failed to return.

The Mosquitoes at Horsham St Faith repeated the same tactics on the second and third 'Thousand Bomber' raids – the second was flown against Essen on 1/2 June, and the third and final raid targeted Bremen on 25/26 June. Flt Lt D A 'George' Parry and Flg Off Victor Robson flew

No 105 Sqn B IVs DZ353/E and DZ367/J formate for the camera at altitude. The latter Mosquito failed to return from a raid to Berlin on 30 January 1943, Sqn Ldr D F W Darling DFC and Flg Off W Wright both losing their lives. DZ353 later served with No 139 Sqn before joining No 627 Sqn, No 8 Group (PFF), as AZ-T on 24 November 1943. On 8 January 1944 it crashed whilst taking off from the Vickers-Armstrong factory at Weybridge following a double gear leg collapse – neither its pilot, Wg Cdr G H B Hutchinson, or navigator, Flg Off F French, were seriously injured. Subsequently repaired and re-coded AZ-B, the veteran bomber was shot down during a raid on the marshalling yards at Rennes on 8 June 1944, with the loss of Flt Lt H 'Harry' Steere DFM and Flg Off K W 'Windy' Gale DFC, RAAF. The former was actually a Spitfire ace from 1940, having served with No 19 Sqn – see Osprey *Aircraft of the Aces 12 Spitfire Mk I/II Aces 1939-41* for further details (*RAF Marham*)

a lone 2 hr 5 min round trip to Essen and dropped their four 500-lb bombs on the target, but smoke again rendered photography impossible. On 25/26 June six No 105 Sqn B Mk IVs flew bombing and photo-recce missions both during and after the third 'Thousand Bomber' raid. These first sorties helped gain experience for the operations that lay ahead.

In between these historic Bomber Command operations taking place, No 139 Sqn was formed at Horsham St Faith on 8 June. Headed by Wg Cdr Peter Shand DFC, the unit was manned by crews and a handful of Mosquito Mk IVs from No 105 Sqn. On 2 July the first joint attack by the two units took place when four aircraft from No 105 Sqn carried out a low-level attack on the U-boat yards at Flensburg whilst two Mosquitoes from No 139 Sqn bombed the same target from high level. Two Mosquitoes were destroyed by German fighters, with Gp Capt J C Mac-Donald being made a PoW and the recently-promoted Wg Cdr A R Oakeshott DFC being killed, along with his navigator Flg Off V F E Treherne DFM. Sqn Ldr Jack Houlston came off the yards pursued by three Fw 190s, whilst Flt Lt G P Hughes was chased by two more after being hit by flak. Both pilots made good their escape by hugging the wave tops and using +12 lbs of boost, which allowed them to outpace their pursuers.

On 11 July six Mosquitoes from No 105 Sqn bombed the Flensburg yards once again as part of a diversion for 44 Lancasters sent to hit the U-boat yards at Danzig. Plt Off Laston returned with part of his fin blown away by flak, while Flt Lt G P Hughes and Flg Off T A Gabe were killed when their Mosquito crashed possibly as a result of flying too low. Sgt Peter W R Rowland was somewhat luckier, however, as he returned to Horsham with pieces of chimney pot lodged in the noseof in DK296!

The rest of July saw a mixture of daylight operations ranging from low and high level bombing to bombing using cloud cover against targets at Ijmuiden, in Holland, and cities throughout Germany. The primary purpose of these raids was to cause the air raid sirens to sound, which resulted in maximum disruption to German industry.

THE EDWARDS ERA

On 3 August 1942 Wg Cdr Hughie I Edwards VC, DFC arrived from Malta to take over command of No 105 Sqn. An Australian who had won the VC for his courageous leadership on a Blenheim raid on Bremen on 4 July 1941, Edwards' arrival coincided with that of Flt Lt Charles Patterson, who had also flown a tour on Blenheims (with No 114 Sqn);

'I was initially sent to a Boston unit, but I managed to get a transfer to Hughie Edwards' squadron. The Mosquito was an exciting new aeroplane, and it was everyones' ultimate aim and ambition to fly it. The rumour got about that it was able to fly unarmed across Europe and get away with it because it was as fast, if not faster, than the enemy fighters. It was such a wonderful aeroplane that it became everyones' dream in our little world to get on to a Mosquito unit. It was certainly mine.

'Edwards was legendary in No 2 Group not only for what he had done, but for what a wonderful individual he was. He made a tremendous impact just by his mere presence. The quality of his leadership was elusive, indescribable. It had something to do with his presence and ability to inspire. He was very imaginative and sensitive, but he placed a premium on efficiency and made it clear that this had two purposes. One was that

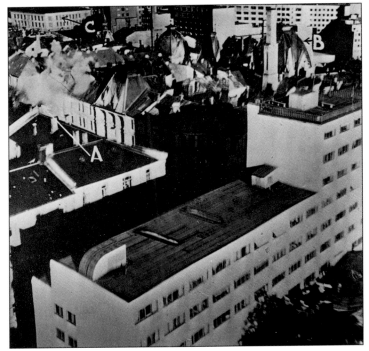

This still was taken from the camera film loaded aboard DK296/G-George crewed by Sqn Ldr George Parry DSO, DFC* and Flg Off Victor 'Robbie' Robson DFC* during the No 105 Sqn raid on the Gestapo HQ in Oslo on 25 September 1942. Parry led the attack by the four Mosquitoes, and this shot shows a direct hit by him (marked 'A' at far left) and the bombs about to burst on the Victoria Terrasse (the ordnance had 11-second delay fuses fitted). 'B' denotes the central domed cupola on which the crews saw the Nazi flag flying, and 'C' marks the large white University building at the top left of the photo. Of the 12 bombs dropped, 5 did not explode and 3 went through the HQ building and detonated outside (*BAe Hatfield via Philip Birtles*)

the target must be hit, secondly, that crews should cover every possibility that would ensure their survival. He studied the tactics of survival combined with success to a greater degree than any other wing commander with whom I came into contact. He inspired crews not by appeals to their sense of duty and purpose, but through the supreme achievement of allowing them to conquer their fear. Far from playing down fear, he brought it into the open and made conquering it the ultimate goal. I didn't find this particular approach in any other leader I came across. He made no attempt to conceal his own fear.

'I think the best example I can give of this was when six crews, led by Edwards, were to go on a high level dawn raid on cities in the Ruhr at a time when casualties on this kind of operation were particularly heavy. We were sitting having breakfast in a naturally very gloomy atmosphere at about five in the morning when Tony Wickham, a young pilot officer going on his first trip, suddenly burst out and said, "I suppose this is a death or glory effort?" Well, pilot officers on their first trip were not supposed to speak on those occasions at all. Most of us reacted with slight disapproval, but Edwards lent forward, looked at him, and said, "There is no glory in it, and that's what makes it so worthwhile." The effect on all of us was electric, and we all went out feeling that we were going on a mission of supreme importance not to the war effort, but to ourselves and to our unit, and to show him that we could do it without thought of glory or reward, for its own sake.

'Mosquito operations were far more ambitious than Blenheim ops, but casualties were lower. When I first joined No 105 Sqn, the operations had not been properly worked out, and no one was sure of what the role for the Mosquito ought to be. It was being used at first for high level work, going out in broad daylight, unescorted, and bombing with a few bombs, and as a nuisance raider after a night raid – the latter idea was that the sirens would go and keep the workers' heads down and out of the factories. Well, it so happened that Bomber Command strategists had not made allowance for the Fw 190, which, at altitude, was slightly faster and certainly more manoeuvrable than the Mosquito Mk IV, which had the speed of the Spitfire. The Fw 190 was marginally faster than a Spitfire at this point in the war, and from July to September 1942, Mosquito casualties were as high as those suffered by Blenheim units performing low level daylight raids a year earlier. There was even talk of the Mosquito having to be written off after all. We still had such enormous faith in this aeroplane, however, and we refused to believe that it could not be made to operate successfully with an acceptable rate of casualties.

'Hughie Edwards had hand-picked his flight commanders and his two deputy flight commanders – my flight commander was Peter Channer. The station commander, Gp Capt (later Air Chief Marshal Sir Wallace) Kyle, and "Eddie", had decided that to get the new crews blooded, they would organise a quick operation. So, on 5 August the target selected was the steelworks at Ijmuiden which, in the Blenheim era, had been regarded as a fierce target. Their idea of a training operation was to send off three new crews, or two new crews under a leader, in the morning, followed by two more in the afternoon against the same target with another leader.

'I was part of the afternoon sortie behind Flt Lt Roy Ralston, a fellow OTU instructor who had already reached a level of reverence throughout the whole of No 2 Group for his tremendous operational record on Blenheims. He was an ex-Halton boy and an ex-sergeant pilot. His navigator was Syd Clayton. Ralston was regarded by many, including Hughie Edwards, as the greatest bomber pilot of all time. He did two tours of daylight operations on Blenheims and another tour at night, before completing another very long operational tour on Mosquitoes at night – he really did four tours. He and Clayton had a record of finding and hitting the target that was certainly unsurpassed, and they did 100 trips together.

'Ijmuiden was a very quick and a fairly easy operation. We crossed the coast, turned north, then south, and there straight ahead of us was the steelworks. A lot of light flak came up. I threw the Mosquito all over the sky, over the roof, and down the other side. Coming out over the coast the heavy flak started up as usual – huge columns of water would go up from shells bursting on the water. You certainly didn't come out in formation, as it was every man for himself.

'A few days later I was told to report to the ops room. My route was up on the map. Even by Mosquito standards I was pretty appalled by what I saw. "Bomber" Harris wanted to know what the weather was like over Germany for a bombing raid that night because the "met" people were rather vague about it. It was a glorious, clear, September day, without a cloud in the sky over England. I was told to fly at 25,000 ft across the Dutch coast and fly straight to Magdeburg. I was then to turn for home, flying north-east past Berlin, up to Rostock and over north-west Denmark to Esbjerg, before returning back to England.

'Apart from anything else, this sortie would push the Mosquito to the limit of its range. I was told that I was the only Allied aircraft operating over Germany, so my chances of getting back seemed slim. To show how bad it was, "Eddie" said he was sorry that he had to send me on the mission, but that it had to be done. With a twinkle in his eye, he said, "You're not married you see, which is a factor we have to take into account".

'The challenge was so great that I didn't really have too much time to worry. As I climbed up to our operational ceiling I felt very "woozy", and I was having to really concentrate on the instruments – somehow my oxygen tube had been disconnected, and my navigator, Sgt Egan, had only noticed it when I was already up at nearly 25,000 ft. Quite suddenly, everything became clear. There in full view was the D utch coast, with Holland spread out like a map in front of me. I felt absolutely normal. Such was "Eddie's" influence that it was purely the thought of him that made me keep going even when I was running out of oxygen at 25,000 ft.

'About half way to Magdeburg Egan quite suddenly screamed, "Snap-

Flt Lt Victor Robson DFC* and Sqn Ldr D A G Parry DSO, DFC* pose in front of G for George of No 105 Sqn at Marham soon after the Oslo raid (*D A G Parry Collection*)

Wg Cdr Hughie Idwal Edwards was born in Mosman Park, Western Australian, to Welsh parents on 1 August 1914. Although he was just 28 years of age when he took command of No 105 Sqn for a second time in August 1942, he had already won the Brtish Empire's highest military medal, the Victoria Cross, for his leadership of nine No 105 Sqn Blenheim IVs during Operation *Wreckage* – a daring daylight bombing raid on Bremen on 4 July 1941. His receipt of the VC made him only the second Australian aviator to receive such an award (the first had been presented to Lt F H McNamara of the AFC during World War 1). On 10 February 1943 Edwards was promoted to temporary group captain and made Station Commander of RAF Binbrook. By 1944 he had taken up an appointment in South East Asia Command, holding a Senior Air Staff Officer rank until the end of 1945. Edwards was awarded the OBE in 1947, and in 1958 he was promoted to air commodore, before retiring from the RAF in 1963. He then returned to his native country and became Governor of West Australia in 1974 – he was knighted during his period in office. Sadly, he was only able to fill this job for nine months before failing health forced his premature retirement. Air Commodore Sir Hughie Idwal Edwards VC, KCMG, CB, DSO, OBE, DFC*, KStJ – Australia's most decorated airman – died on 5 August 1982 (*RAAF*)

pers!" (enemy fighters). I threw the Mosquito into a vertical turning dive, thinking, "Oh my God, we've had it now". Then Egan told me, "Oh, I'm very sorry, it's only a fly!" I was so relieved and I resumed the flight. At our height you had to watch your back all the time so as to ensure that you where not letting out vapour trails. If you were, you had to drop height immediately. We carried on to Magdeburg in glorious blue sky – you could see for a hundred miles. When we turned north-east, mercifully we ran into cloud, which carried on till we were just short of Rostock, which was the most dangerous part of the trip. After we came out of this cloud there was blue sky and the Baltic spread out beneath us. We got to Esbjerg, and with a sigh of relief I dived down to sea level, and safety. It was nearly dusk when we got back to Horsham St Faith. A slightly flustered Hughie Edwards met us. He had heard nothing and had written us off.'

On 29 August Wg Cdr Edwards and his navigator, Flg Off H H 'Bladder' Cairns DFC, were part of two-aircraft formation from No 105 Sqn that bombed a power station at Pont-Ö-Vendin. During their return flight the Mosquitoes were attacked by a dozen Fw 190s some 40 miles inside enemy territory. The fighters approached from head-on, before turning around behind the fleeing bombers to give chase from astern. However, the Mosquitoes easily outpaced their assailants, but not before both aircraft had been struck (Edwards' Mosquito was hit in the port engine) by enemy fire, forcing the OC to belly land at Lympne, in Kent, whilst the second Mk IV crash-landed at Oakington, in Cambridgeshire.

On 19 September No 105 Sqn flew their boldest operation so far when six crews attempted the first daylight Mosquito raid on Berlin. Sgt N Booth (in DZ312) and Flt Sgt Monaghan (in DK336) were forced to return early, while Flt Lt Roy Ralston and Flg Off Sydney Clayton bombed Hamburg after finding Berlin covered by cloud. Flt Lt George Parry and Flt Lt Victor Robson (in DK339) were intercepted on two occasions by Fw 190s but managed to evade them. Parry jettisoned his bombs near Hamburg and turned for home, heading back across the north coast of Germany into Holland. At 1000 ft just off the Dutch coast, two Bf 109s attacked, and although one of them scored hits, Parry dropped to sea level and outran them. DK326/M, crewed by Sqn Ldr N H F Messervy DFC and Plt Off F Holland, was shot down by *Schwarmführer*, Oberfeldwebel Anton-Rudolf 'Toni' Piffer, of 2./JG 1 between Wesermunde and Stade, near Wilhelmshaven, which meant that only Wt Off C R K Bools and Sgt G W Jackson (who were both latter killed in action on 9 October 19 42) actually succeeded in bombing the 'Big City'.

Six days later, on 25 September, No 105 Sqn flew a momentous daylight raid against the Gestapo Headquarters in Oslo following a request by the Norwegian government in exile in London. Leading the special operation was George Parry, who was now a squadron leader, with his navigator, Flg Off 'Robbie' Robson. The remaining three crews involved were Flt Lt Pete Rowland and Flg Off Richard Reilly, Flg Off Alec Bristow and Plt Off Bernard Marshall, and Flt Sgt Gordon Carter and Sgt William Young. In order to shorten the mission distance, the four Mosquitoes were firstly flown up to Leuchars, in Scotland, where each aircraft was refuelled and loaded with four 11-second delayed action 500-lb bombs, prior to setting out across the North Sea. The operation involved a round trip of 1100 miles, with an air time of four and three-quarter hours – the longest Mosquito operation hitherto flown. The bombers crossed the North Sea at heights of between 50 to 100 ft to avoid interception, and crews used dead reckoning along the entire route.

Despite the low flying, a pair of Fw 190s from 3./JG 5 intercepted the Mosquitoes inbound, forcing Carter's aircraft to crash into a lake. Rowland and Reilly were pursued by the other Fw 190 until the latter clipped a tree and had to break off the attack. At least four bombs entered the Gestapo HQ, one of which remained inside and failed to detonate, whilst the other three crashed through the opposite wall before exploding. On the night of 26 September 1942, listeners to the BBC Home Service heard that a new aircraft – the Mosquito – had been officially revealed for the first time by the RAF, and that four had made a roof top raid on Oslo.

Soon after this mission Horsham St Faith was allocated to the USAAF as a Liberator base, so on 29 September Nos 105 and 139 Sqns began moving to their new station at Marham. The latter airfield had just been transferred from No 3 to No 2 Group, and would play a leading role in Mosquito operations until March 1944. F/L Charles Patterson recalls:

'Shortly after we moved to Marham the great glamour period of No 105 Sqn began. Edwards changed the tactics from high level daylight to low level daylight, bombing about 20 minutes before dark when it was light enough to identify the target, and then coming back under cover of growing darkness. This became the standard operation with the Mosquitoes, and it was highly successful. We flew some audacious raids deep into Europe in this way, and never got intercepted by fighters. Such losses as we had were to light flak – when crossing the coasts in the wrong place, or going over a defended area, that was always the risk you took.'

Wg Cdr Hughie Edwards (at rear) and his regular navigator, Flt Lt C H H 'Bladder' Cairns, prepare to climb aboard their Mosquito at RAF Marham in preparation for their next sortie in late 1942 (*via Philip Birtles*)

THE 'SHALLOW DIVERS'

On 2 October 1942 six Mosquitoes from No 105 Sqn attacked Liége using a new type of tactic that would drastically improve the aircraft's bombing accuracy against pin-point targets. Apart from the 'traditional' low-level attack, crews were introduced to the 'shallow diving' method, the latter attack seeing the crew zoom down from 2000 to 1500 ft just prior to arriving over the target – their bombs were then released once they were at the lower altitude. With the availability of more B Mk IVs in 1943, this tactic would, on occasion, be used by the 'shallow divers' in conjunction with the first wave, who went in at low-level proper with 11-second delayed-action bombs. When this occurred, up to 20 Mosquitoes could cross the target almost simulataneously, as Charles Patterson vividly recalls;

'During October/November 1942 I did a number of exciting operations deep into Germany, going out at high level and coming back at low level, which was a most exhilerating experience. My splendid navigator was taken sick and removed, and I had to take whatever navigator was going, which usually meant one whom no-one else wanted. Having a navigator who (when flying low level in poor light), for 80 per cent of the time, hadn't the faintest idea where he was, added somewhat to the excitement. It also placed a much greater strain on my initiative and judgement.

'In the middle of November we all started to practice low level formation bombing day after day, whenever the weather permitted, for what we understood would be one of the major raids. The whole group was going to be involved, which meant that Venturas, Bostons and Mosquitoes would all have to operate together and arrive over the target simultaneously. Their differing operational speeds posed a planning headache, but this was not the worry of ordinary pilots like myself.

'On the morning of 20 November, Wg Cdr Edwards introduced me to Flg Off Jimmy Hill who, it was explained, was from the RAF Film Unit. He had a cine camera which was to be fitted into my Mosquito (DK338 'O-Orange'), and I was to take him on a low level recon-

No 105 Sqn's Sqn Ldr Roy Ralston DSO, DFM and Flt Lt Syd Clayton DFC, DFM are seen on 9 December 1942 following a very successful bombing raid which saw them lead two other B Mk IVs in a 'skip bombing' raid on the mouth of a French railway tunnel. The attack was designed to cause damage to both the tunnel and the track on the other side, thus making it difficult for the Germans to effect repairs (*via Philip Birtle*s)

naissance of the Schelde Estuary. We would take a film of the route down the estuary, which the raiders would subsequently use on the forthcoming "big operation". This cine film would serve as an important navigational aid in the briefing of crews – particularly the lead navigators. When the actual operation took place a cine camera would be carried for the first time. The powers-that-be told me that I would have to navigate myself, but that Hill had done a navigator's course.

'All we had to do was fly down the Schelde Estuary just over the Dutch mainland near Woensdrecht fighter airfield and back again, but we could not go in at low level. We had to go in at about 300 ft in order to get the correct angle for the cine camera to give a perspective of the islands ahead. By luck, and by dead reckoning, we arrived at the right point of entry, and Hill went down into the nose with his film camera. It was all very peaceful. We whizzed down the Schelde Estuary and crossed the mainland, and when I could see the hangars of Woensdrecht airfield on the horizon I turned sharply about and came home again. Well, they developed

this film with a great deal of excitement. Both Gaumont British News and my pet spaniel were waiting when I landed, and the latter ended up on the news as well! Sadly, it soon became quite plain when the film was put on the projector that it was useless to navigators because the islands ahead looked just like any other islands along the Dutch coast.'

On 1 May 1943 Charles Patterson's DK338 took off for a raid on Eindhoven but lost an engine soon after take off and crashed near Marham, killing Flg Off O W Thompson DFC, RNZAF and Flg Off W J Horne DFC. The aircraft had successfully completed 23 sorties.

OPERATION *OYSTER*

On 6 December 1942 Operation *Oyster* saw 84 Mosquito, Boston and Ventura bombers from No 2 Group attack the Philips Stryp Group main works and the Emmasingel valve and lamp factory in Eindhoven, Holland. Ten Mosquitoes (eight Mk IVs of No 105 Sqn and two from No 139 Sqn), led by Wg Cdr Hughie Edwards VC, DFC made a shallow diving attack on the Stryp works, while the other bombers dropped their ordnance from low level. Sqn Ldr J E Houlston AFC, DFC of No 139

Top and above
The No 2 Group attack on the Philips Stryp Group main works at Eindhoven, Holland, is seen in progress on 6 December 1942. Some 84 bombers, including 11 B Mk IVs (eight from No 105 Sqn and two from No 139), took part in Operation *Oyster*, as the mission was code-named. The Mosquito force, led by Wg Cdr Hughie Edwards VC, DFC made a shallow diving attack on the Stryp works, while the other bombers dropped their ordnance from low level. No 139 Sqn's Sqn Ldr J E Houlston AFC, DFC carried out bomb damage assessment in the immediate aftermath of the raid (*via GMS*)

No 105 Sqn line up at Marham on 11 December 1942. The closest aircraft, DZ360/A, failed to return from Termonde just 11 days later, with the loss of Flt Sgt J E Cloutier and Sgt A C Foxley; DZ353/E was lost on 9 June 1944 (see page 8); DZ367/J was downed during a raid to Berlin on 30 January 1943; DK336/P lost its starboard engine returning from a raid on Copenhagen on 27 January 1943, then struck a balloon cable and a tree and crashed at Yaxham, in Norfolk, killing Sgt R Clare and Flg Off E Doyle; DZ378/K was withdrawn from service after only two sorties following damage inflicted on 20 December 1942; and PZ379/H was lost on 17 August 1943 whilst flying with No 139 Sqn on a diversionary mission to Berlin for the famous Peenemünde raid – the Mosquito, which was downed by a nightfighter, carried both Flg Off A S Cook (an American pilot from Wichita Falls, Texas) and navigator, Sgt D A H Dixon, to their deaths

Sqn carried out bomb damage assessment. Charles Patterson again;

'Operationally, the Philips works raid from a Mosquito point of view was regarded as a comparatively straightforward target – nothing to get terribly frightened about, and something we would have taken in our stride as part of routine operations. I flew in the second formation of four Mosquitoes (in DZ414 'O for Orange') as No 3 to Sqn Ldr George Parry, who was a very famous Mosquito pilot, and one of our flight commanders. We followed Edwards' formation of six.

'Our attack was supposedly timed so that we didn't get involved with either the Venturas or Bostons. Our concern was that should we get tangled up with either type, we would have to reduce speed, which of course from a Mosquito point of view was dangerous because we had no defensive armament. We were to fly to somewhere just south of Eindhoven, turn to port, and then attack the target. The Mosquitoes were to climb to 1500 ft just short of the target and then shallow dive on to it because it was assumed that Bostons would have hit it at low level before us – Hill would film the target with his cine camera. This sounded an interesting thing to do because for once there would be a chance of seeing what we'd done afterwards.

'We flew across the Dutch coast at low level. The thing I remember most clearly was looking across my port wing tip and seeing Fw 190s literally in a line taking off from Woensdrecht to intercept us. They only looked about 200-300 yards away – it was actually about half a mile. They looked so normal, just like Spitfires taking off in England, that it was hard to believe they were coming up to kill you. We had to slow right down as we found ourselves getting involved with some Venturas. We ended up not far above our stalling speed as we tried to get behind them.'

Showing both coolness and decisiveness, Sqn Ldr George Parry and his No 2, Flt Lt Bill Blessing, broke away so as to draw the Fw 190s onto themselves, but they eventually lost them as they accelerated to full speed. Parry later rejoined the formation, but Blessing had to return to base.

'The Fw 190s couldn't resist it when they saw these two turn round, and they duly fell for Parry's deception, leaving us alone. The Mk IV was slower than the Fw 190 at 20,000 ft, but at deck level it was 5 mph faster.

'There were no more fighter interceptions. Ahead of me I saw the front formation of Mosquitoes in the distance already climbing up to 1500 ft, so I immediately took my formation up as fast as I could in order to catch

Edwards' formation. We caught up about two to three miles south of Eindhoven. He banked over to port and started to dive down on the Philips works in the centre of the town. The moment I turned to port I could see the factory prominantly standing out right in the centre of Eindhoven. We all went down in a shallow dive at full throttle, and at the appropriate moment dropped the bombs. As I went across the Philips works the factory seemed to erupt in a cloud of smoke and flashes. It looked as though the whole thing had been completely destroyed.

'In the distance I could see masses of Bostons whizzing about across the trees at low level to port. I came straight down to ground level. Now the Mosquitoes split up and we all had to come home separately. It was now noon on a lovely sunny day, with virtually no cloud, so I set off across the Dutch countryside at high speed. I decided not to follow the given route out, which was towards the coast of Holland and out into the North Sea. I decided that that was where the fighters would be, waiting for the main formation, so I therefore turned north towards the Zuider Zee. Plt Off J E O'Grady, who was on his first trip (with Sgt G W Lewis), latched on to me to see him home. He followed me all the way up the Zuider Zee, and I knew we'd made it when we whizzed over the Causeway at about 20 ft.

'I turned to port to come out between Den Helder and Texel. This was a mistake on my part because the light flak sites at Den Helder and on the southern tip of Texel were sufficiently close enough to hit you should you fly between them. I therefore had to cross a belt of light flak and weaving tracer as I flew between the two islands, but I emerged unscathed. I took the usual evasive action, and the Mosquito behind appeared to be perfectly all right. However, when we were about six minutes out into the North Sea, Hill said, "He's gone into the sea!" At first I could not believe what he was saying because we were now some 30 miles out to sea, but

B Mk IV Series II DZ367/J of No 139 Sqn is bombed up in preparation for a raid – note that the aircraft's shrouded exhausts have scorched the cowlings). One of three No 139 Sqn aircraft sent to bomb Berlin in an attempt to disrupt a speech being made by Nazi propaganda minister, Dr Joseph Goebbels, on the afternoon of 30 January 1943, this Mosquito was lost (along with its crew) during the daring daylight raid (via Shuttleworth Collection)

when I turned round and went back it was only too true. All that remained of the Mosquito was a big, boiling, cauldron of water. O'Grady was a nice, cheerful, young Canadian. I'd known him as a pupil at OTU at Upwood when I was an instructor. He only looked about 16 – I suppose he was about 20. I momentarily felt guilty, for if I'd done something different, and he hadn't followed me, he'd still be alive.

'When the film was developed half of it was spoiled in the laboratory, which made both Hughie Edwards and I absolutely livid (in total, more than 60 tons of bombs had hit the Philips factories, which were very badly damaged, but 14 aircraft had been lost). Unbeknown to me, Eindhoven turned out to be the beginning of a new operational role that I was to perform for a long time. A month later I was sent to Hatfield to test fly three Mosquitoes and pick out one that I thought had the best performance. Whilst I was there Sir Geoffrey de Havilland treated me as an honoured guest. I chose DZ414, which was allotted to the RAF Film Unit (FU). Coded 'O-Orange', I was to fly it for 20,000 of its 24,000 miles.'

Charles Patterson then returned to Marham, and No 105 Squadron;

'Christmas came and went and the weather turned bad in January 1943, so I only did two ops. We all settled down to practice for a low level daylight attack on the Burmeister and Wain submarine building yards at Copenhagen, but at this time there was a sudden sweep of rumours. A change in the Mosquito force was planned, and any crew could volunteer to join a new formation in Bomber Command called the Pathfinders. It would mean promotion and an interesting new job. I had now been four months on my second tour so I thought I would try a change.

'I duly joined No 109 Sqn at Wyton, but I discovered that the Mosquito was going to fly on instruments at 30,000 ft at night and mark targets using *Oboe*. The attitude of everyone there was simply antipathetic to my outlook because they regarded themselves as the elite, whereas none of them had actually flown operations that were anything like as dangerous, daring or comprehensive as we'd been doing in No 2 Group – I didn't much care for the chaps there, and I certainly didn't like the job. I undertook one night film operation using DZ414 during my time as a Pathfinder, but this was a futile effort because to the public, every target at night looked the same. So it was decided to return the FU Mosquito back to No 105 Sqn and make low level daylight films with it instead.'

The raid on the Burmeister and Wain works went ahead on 27 January 1943, with Wg Cdr Edwards leading nine B Mk IVs of Nos 105 and 139

No 139 Sqn armourers check that the recently loaded bombs have been correctly fitted into the belly of Mosquito DZ464 at Marham in the early spring of 1943. This aircraft was lost just days later on 21 May 1943 when it was downed by flak over the French coast following a bombing raid on the locomotive sheds at Orleans. Former acting squadron OC, Sqn Ldr V R G Harcourt DFC, RCAF, and his navigator, Wt Off O J Friendly DFM RCAF, were killed in the crash

Mid February 1943 became known as the 'Great Tours Derby' for the aircrew of Nos 105 and 139 Sqns. On the afternoon of 14 February the engine sheds in the French city were attacked from low level by six of the ten Mosquitoes despatched by No 139 Sqn The following evening, 12 Mosquitoes from No 105 Sqn bombed the Tours goods depot in a low-level raid, and on the 18th a dozen B Mk IVs made a shallow diving attack on the same target (pictured here) – two aircraft aborted and one Mosquito failed to return (*DH via GMS*)

Sqns. Light flak from ships positioned along the coast bracketed the formation on the way in, leaving Flt Lt J Gordon DFC and Flg Off R G Hayes DFC thinking that their aircraft had been hit when the trailing edge of their starboard wing became enveloped in blue smoke. However, Gordon had actually clipped a telegraph line whilst carrying out evasive action in an effort to put the German gunners off their aim. He quickly turned around and headed home with a damaged port aileron – both men were subsequently killed in a crash whilst attempting to return on one engine from an operation to Leverkusen on 5 November 1943.

Edwards and Cairns found their target just as they too were on the point of returning, but they swiftly dropped their bombs and broke for the sea – and home. Light flak around the yards was intense, claiming the Mosquito flown by Sgts J G Dawson and R H Cox – Edwards' aircraft returned with two holes in the starboard nacelle.

On 30 January Mosquitoes bombed Berlin in two attacks, the first (in the morning) involving three Mk IVs of No 105 Sqn, led by Sqn Ldr 'Reggie' W Reynolds and Plt Off E B 'Ted' Sismore, and the second (in the afternoon) a trio of aircraft from No 139 Sqn. Both raids were timed to disrupt speeches being given at the main broadcasting station by Reichsmarschall Herman Göring and Dr Joseph Goebbels. No 105 Sqn arrived over Berlin at exactly 1100 hours, their bombs disrupting Göring's speech for over an hour. Sadly, the second raid was not as successful, with Sqn Ldr D F W Darling DFC being shot down and killed.

Whilst all this was going on Charles Patterson eased his way back into operations with No 105 Sqn again after his brief sojourn in No 8 Group;

'They had been going "great-guns" during February-March, demonstrating how the Mosquito could go in at zero feet on a regular basis and

Precision bombing at its best – the U-boat Supply Depot at Rennes after the low level attack by 16 Mosquitoes of Nos 105 and 139 Sqns on 26 February 1943. Leading the raid was No 105 Sqn's newly-appointed OC, Wg Cdr G P Longfield (with navigator Flt Lr R F Millns), in DZ365/V. Both men were killed when their aircraft collided with DZ413/K, crewed by Flg Offs S G Kimmel and H N Kirkland, RCAF, whilst attempting to avoid flak over the target area (*via GMS*)

get back with at least an acceptable rate of casualties. Then No 139 Sqn began specialising in a new form of attack, climbing to 1500 ft and doing a shallow dive down on to the target in the wake of the low level Mosquitoes from No 105 Sqn. The latter unit now had a new squadron commander called John Wooldridge – a rather flamboyant character who had done an enormous number of trips in heavy bombers. He had a DFC and two Bars, and a large moustache!'

Hughie Edwards had left No 105 Sqn in February to take up a post at HQ Bomber Command, but his successor, Wg Cdr G P Longfield, only lasted a matter of days as he was killed in a mid-air collision on 26 February 1943. Wg Cdr John de Lacy Wooldridge DFC, DFM assumed command of the unit on 17 March and went on to lead No 105 Sqn on many low level raids – for which he was duly awarded a DSO and a bar to his DFC. Charles Patterson again;

'During the next two or three months I went off on a few "low levels", one of which was a very long one indeed (on a fine afternoon on 2 May) to the railway repair workshops at Thionville, near Metz. We flew at low level in eight Mosquitoes led by Reggie Reynolds, who was a new flight commander with Wellington experience, and Ted Sismore, who'd developed into an absolutely brilliant navigator. We flew ar low level across the Channel. Of course, flying the FU Mosquito I was always near the back – three from the end, flying No 5, with two aircraft in starboard echelon. We were always in a starboard echelon because the aircraft's response to the throttles opening and shutting was so lethargic. This meant that the Mosquito could not decelerate safely, only accelerate, so we always flew in echelon rather than a vic. This problem also negated any chance the pilot had of manoeuvering at low level when on the outside of a turn.

'As we came up over the cliffs we encountered some light flak. It seemed to be getting very near to me, so when I judged that the moment was right, I pulled on the stick and went up about 100 ft. As I did so, the flak shot under me and hit the starboard engine of the chap to my left, causing the aircraft to emit a large black cloud of smoke. The crew then feathered the engine and went back home on one. I resumed my normal position.

'We flew right across northern France, north-west of Paris, and down to Soissons – mile after mile at low level, across the green fields of France. Then we banked due east to come up to Thionville, which lay some 20 miles south, before turning to port in an effort to avoid any chance of us missing the target by flying too far north or south. These were always the tactics used, and of course we did "dog legs", never flying in one direction for more than 20 minutes. As a result, we reached Thionville without a shot being fired. We raced up on the target, with Reynolds in the leading aircraft opening up the throttles. He wouldn't go across the target flat out (the leader wouldn't do that), but he'd go up to about 300, and then he'd give the order to open the bomb doors. Then the target came up and everyone went for it. You were over it and gone in a flash. We achieved complete surprise, which allowed us to get across the target and deliver our bombs right on the mark. The last pilot over said he thought he saw a gun open fire.

'Now the really interesting part of the trip arrived. Instead of turning back north-west to fly across France and Belgium, we carried out the highly imaginative idea of heading due north, knowing that the Germans would assume that we must be coming back across north-west France – they would be sending their fighters down to that area to meet us before it got dark, so to fox them we flew north. It was an extraordinary sensation flying across the mountains of Luxembourg and the forests of the Ardennes at low level,

An enemy flak gun emplacement opens up on a Mosquito during a low level attack by four B Mk IVs of No 105 Sqn on the Stork Diesel Works at Hengelo, in Holland, on 28 February 1943. The flying debris in the foreground is from a bomb that had just burst through the roof of the Manemeyer electrical and mechanical equipment factory. The train passing behind the flak gun emplacement is travelling along the Derventer to Zwolle railway line (via Philip Birtles)

before crossing into Germany. It seemed endless, and then in the gathering gloom we suddenly shot across the banks of the Rhine and up across Holland – I came out between Ameland and Vlieland. Flying over the Causeway at the top of the Zuider Zee, I knew I was on course for home.'

BOMBS ON THE 'BIG CITY'

Just prior to the Thionville raid, No 105 Sqn was involved in a hastily arranged surprise bombing attack on Berlin on the night of 20/21 April 1943. One of the pilots involved was Charles Patterson;

'The primary reason for this mission was to "celebrate" Hitler's birthday by delivering a suitable "present" to him. As this date coincided with a full moon, Bomber Command planners had enough sense to know that the Mosquito possessed the range to get to Berlin and back in moonlight conditions. Eight of us went on this attack. It was the most brilliant moonlight night, and the flight was a very long one – over four hours, of which roughly three would be spent over enemy territory. We had to constantly keep a lookout for fighters because the moon was so bright, weaving and turning so that our navigators could look back for them. The moon would catch and reflect on the wings and on the perspex, and looking down, all the lakes were lit up with the reflection of the moon. I don't think that this trip worried anybody, It certainly didn't worry me. To go over Germany at high level at night in a Mosquito seemed almost as safe as flying over England, provided you kept out of the way of any fighters.

'Berlin was not difficult to pick out thanks to the vast "blackness" of the city and the Potsdam lakes. I was at about 18,000 ft and settled down to

Wg Cdr John de Lacy Wooldridge DFC*, DFM, took over command of No 105 Sqn on 17 March 1943. He is seen here posing in the emergency roof exit hatch of his personal Mosquito B Mk IV, *KNAVE OF DIAMONDS*. Note the two-piece front windscreen, which was soon replaced by a bullet-proof fighter style flat windscreen, and the direct vision panel (forward of the blister), which opened inwards on each side. Wooldridge joined the RAF in 1938 and flew two tours on heavy bombers (including 32 ops on the ill-fated Manchester with Nos 61, 207 and 106 Sqns) prior to taking command of No 105 Sqn. He survived the war only to die in a car accident in 1958 (*via Philip Birtles*)

do a straight and level run. The only thing about this attack was that we felt it was slightly "second class" when compared with the daylight raid that we had done a few months before. We resented being sent on such a mission as it was not taken very seriously by Bomber Command.

'Suddenly, there were flashes and black puffs of flak. I remember thinking "this is not what you get in a Mosquito – you're too fast for this sort of thing" – and then just before I dropped my bombs there was a violent bump. I thought it outrageous that one could be downed at night in a Mosquito. It was just not done. It was unsporting and not good form at all.

'Anyway, we turned round and weaved our way back across northern Germany and over the Dutch coast in the direction of home – we were bathed in brilliant moonlight throughout the operation. We had one loss – Wg Cdr Peter Shand, OC No 139 Sqn (and his navigator, Plt Off C D Handley DFM), who we subsequently heard had been downed (by Ober-leutnant Lothar Linke of IV./NJG 1) on the way home.

'Once back on the ground, we were debriefed and went to bed. When I went up to the flights the next morning I was asked if I had realised that I had been hit the night before? I said, "No. I had a bump and realised that there had been a burst fairly close. I didn't know I had been hit. I suppose there are just a few tiny little holes in the wing or something?" They said, "Oh no, You've virtually had it". A piece of shrapnel had gone right through the tail of the Mosquito where the elevator wires all link up with the tailplane and the rudder. All but one of these wires had been totally severed, the sole intact strand on a single control line allowing me fly the Mosquito as if nothing had happened. I was unaware that anything was wrong at all as the aircraft had handled perfectly.

'Although we were ignorant of it at the time, this night attack was to set the pattern for Mosquito operations for the rest of the war. Harris and his Bomber Command staff were very taken with the idea that they could send a force of bombers to Berlin any night of the year, regardless of the moon, and it resulted in Nos 105 and 139 Sqns being retained in Bomber Command when No 2 Group went into the 2nd Tactical Air Force – this was a severe setback for both units.

'After Berlin, I went on one quick trip to France on 24 April, during which we were intercepted by Fw 190s some 50 miles south of the Normandy coast. Three of us were going to attack Tours, and the leader spotted the fighters and told us to turn and run for it with the call, "Snappers! Return to base". So we all split up and went flat out, racing across Normandy at absolutely full throttle right on the ground with these Fw 190s haring after us, but not quite able to get within striking range, trailing us all the way up to the coast. Two Fw 190s flew slap across my nose – if I had been in a fighter-bomber Mosquito I could have fired straight at them. I was very amused to note that when their leader saw us, he opened up his throttles and fled, rather than turning back into us and attacking. This behaviour was very significant as it was evi-dence of the virtual collapse of morale within the Luftwaffe day-fighter force – this became even more prevalent as the war went on, the German fighter force having to rely on terribly raw and inexperienced young pilots.'

THE JENA RAID

On 27 May 1943 an operation was laid on for Nos 105 and 139 Sqns which would mark the end of the great low level daylight raids for RAF Bomber Command. Participating crews were unaware of the mission's significance at the time, as Charles Patterson recalls;

'We were all called into the crewroom at about 2 o'clock one afternoon and told that there was to be a major operation. We saw the red route marker ribbon running longer than we'd ever considered right down into south-east Germany, near Leipzig. The target was soon revealed as the Zeiss optical lens works at Jena which, at that time, was engaged almost exclusively in making periscopes for submarines.'

The operation called for eight B Mk IVs of No 105 Sqn to hit the Zeiss factory while six No 139 Sqn Mosquitoes bombed the nearby Schott Glass Works. Patterson again;

'It gave me a great sense of anticipation and excitement that such a tremendously long trip was going to be undertaken, but equally did not cause me undue alarm because it was so deep into Germany – an area that had never seen daylight flying aircraft before. We rather assumed that by going "deep down" not only could we achieve a great deal of surprise, but there might not be much AA fire around the factory – we also believed that any flak sites in the area would be manned by inexperienced gunners.

'The BBC came to do an outside broadcast of the whole thing. The briefing was both long and complicated. It meant flying at low level over enemy territory for well over three hours – a good two-and-a-quarter hours of which would be in broad daylight. I was the Film Unit pilot, and Flt Sgt Leigh Howard was my cameraman-navigator. When the briefing was over we went back to the hangars, after which followed an extraordinarily long period of waiting for the right time to go down to the aircraft

This daring roof top attack on the St Joseph Locomotive Works in Nantes on 23 March 1943 was timed to perfection so as to allow factory workers to have vacated the site prior to the first bombs being dropped. The raid was carried out by three B Mk IVs of No 105 Sqn, led by Wg Cdr Peter Shand DFC, and eight aircraft from No 139 Sqn, led by Sqn Ldr Bill Blessing DSO, DFC, RAAF (who was later killed in action on 7 July 1944 on a 'Path Finder Force' marking sortie over Caen). Shand led two more outstandingly successful attacks against the molybdenum mines at Knaben, in Norway, on 3 March, and on Eindhoven some 27 days later. He and his navigator, Plt Off C D Handley DFM, were lost on the night bombing attack on Berlin on 20/21 April 1943 when their Mosquito was shot down by Oberleutnant Lothar Linke of IV./NJG 1 over Ijsselmeer during their return trip home (*via Philip Birtles*)

Wg Cdr R W Reynolds DSO, DFC (at right) assumes command of No 139 Sqn (note the unit's 'Jamaica Squadron' crest above the doorway at RAF Marham) in May 1943 from acting OC, Sqn Ldr V R G Harcourt, RCAF (*RAF Marham*)

and strap in. It was a gloriously clear and hot, but slightly misty, late May evening. The timing of the take-offs to get the whole formation into the air had to be precise, so there had been a synchronisation of watches. We all settled into our aircraft ten minutes prior to start up so as to ensure that everyone was aboard.

'The time had arrived. Wg Cdr Reynolds was going to lead with Sismore. We saw the flash of his exhaust and his engines started. At 7 o'clock engines fired up around the perimeter and everybody taxied out. Forming up on these trips was a lengthy business, the leader circling slowly round the airfield waiting for everybody to get airborne and catch up. Here I was again with this damn camera, going on another major trip at the end of my second tour, and flying near the back of not the first, but the second, formation.

'The two formations swept across the hangars and the airfield at low level, which made for an impressive sight, and quite an exhilerating experience for the crews themselves. We settled down for the long flight across to Jena in clear daylight, as it was certainly a good two hours before dusk. The Dutch coast was crossed with no difficulty, but at the Zuider Zee we suddenly found ourselves flying slap into a vast fleet of little brown-sailed fishing vessels. In front of me the whole formation broke up and weaved in and around them, before we settled down again. On past the Ruhr and down near Kassel we went, then on into the Thuringian mountains, where the Möhne and Eder dams are. Even then we were only two-thirds of the way. You felt you were in a different world which has no end and will go on forever. On and on over the trees, fields and rising ground we went, mile after mile. Then, suddenly, my navigator drew my attention to something. I looked across the starboard wingtip and could clearly see Münster cathedral some miles away – the interesting thing was that I was looking *up* at the towers, not down on them!

'We carried on past Kassel, then, suddenly, we came across all the floods of the Möhne dam raid which had taken place just ten days before. For 20 minutes there was nothing but floods. It was fascinating to see, and confirmed in our minds what an enormous success the raid must have been. We flew between the Möhne and Eder dams and suddenly came over a mountain ridge and there was a dam beneath us. On the far side the front formation was just topping the far ridge when flak opened up – it didn't look very serious. However, an enormous ball of flame rolled down the mountainside, which was obviously an aircraft, and it wasn't long before that I learnt that *two* Mosquitoes had collided (crewed by Flt Lt

Sutton/Flg Off Morris and Flg Off Openshaw/Sgt Stonestreet, both from No 139 Sqn). Whether one was hit by flak, or the presence of enemy fire had caused one of the pilots to take his eyes off what he was doing and fly into the Mosquito next to him, nobody will ever know, but two had gone.

'We flew on over the mountainous country, along ridges and down long valleys with houses on both sides. We saw a man open his front door on my starboard wingtip and look out to see us flashing past his house. We then saw the door slam in a flash as we whipped past.

Suddenly, the weather began to deteriorate, which had not been forecast. I think everybody was assuming that we'd soon fly out of it, but it got worse and and we were still over mountains. We now began to fly right into clouds. Flying in formation in cloud and knowing you're right in the centre of Germany gives you a rather lonely feeling. Blessing put on his navigation lights to try and enable us to keep formation, and everybody followed suit. I was very nervous about flying on instruments in cloud, and although I did my best to keep the next aircraft in view, I lost him. I found myself flying alone, so I wondered what was going to happen to everybody else. I assumed that perhaps the whole formation had split up. The only thing to do was to fly on by dead reckoning. When I came out of the cloud the visibility was poor. It was grey and gloomy, and Howard had no idea where he was. The only thing to do was to turn for home and see if I could pick up something which was worth bombing.

'So I set off, lost in the sense that I'd no idea where we actually were. The only thing to do was to stick to the flight plan and steer north-east to come up north of Hanover, by which time it should be getting dark, and then fly west across the Hanoverian plain into the night. I'd only been flying a very short time when suddenly I approached what was clearly a very

B Mk IV DZ464/'C-Charlie' (in the background) of No 139 Sqn was the only one of four Mosquitoes to escape unharmed after being chased by two Fw 190s following an attack on Malines on 11 April 1943. As mentioned on page 18, this aircraft was subsequently lost on its 17th operation on 21 May 1943 during a raid on the locomotive sheds at Orleans (*RAF Marham*)

large town. In view of the low cloud base at about 800-1000 ft, and the limited visibility, I felt quite safe. If any fighters appeared, I could pop into the cloud. There was no sign of a factory – it was a residential town, so I assumed there wasn't much flak about. I flew right round and noticed a large railway station in the centre, which our maps told us was Weimar.

'I pointed the nose slightly down, opened up to full throttle and went into a medium steep dive straight at the station. I opened the bomb doors and dropped my ordnance straight into the station from about 200 ft. I couldn't miss. All hell broke loose, as light flak came flashing and whizzing up. I twisted and dodged until we got to the edge of town, and then I descended to rooftop height and ran up a valley flanked by green hills. The flak went on, and I thought that it would never stop. After a time you're supposed to leave flak in your wake, and to still have it going on when I'd dodged so much seemed to me to be most unfair. I began to get worried, for if it went on like this they would hit me eventually.

'More tracer came up from the sides of the hills. I pulled the stick back and yawed to port, then pushed it down and yawed to starboard, trying never to keep a constant pattern of behaviour. Then at last we emerged from this ordeal. I felt rather shaken by it. I didn't even bother to consult my navigator because I knew he'd be palpitating like a jelly. He was a pre-war Pinewoods or Denham studio cameraman who'd suddenly found himself in this horrifying position. There I was in the middle of Germany, unsure of my position, and having no clear idea of what course to steer to get home, which was a hell of a long way away. It was quite a daunting prospect, but there was no point in panicking. This was the sole occasion during my wartime flying that I felt both isolated and apprehensive.

'We set off on the right course, flying long enough to get north of Hamelin, which was defended, and finally the bad weather evaporated. By this time I was out over the familiar North Hamburg Plain again, and I at least knew that I was flying in the right direction. The light was now beginning to fade, and I knew that before long it would be too dark for the fighters. When flying west you were heading straight into the sunset, thus it took longer to get dark. However, by the time we crossed the Dutch frontier it was virtually night, so I could come up to 400-500 ft to avoid obstacles – but not before I'd had a few minutes at low level. Over Holland – much more than Belgium – when low flying aircraft were heard they were probably Mosquitoes, and the Dutch would run to the doors of their little houses and open and shut them signalling a flashing light of welcome to us. I took no notice of the route which had been set for me by

B Mk IV Series II DZ467 GB-P of No 105 Sqn was on its 19th operational sortie when it failed to return from the epic long distance raid on the Zeiss Optical Factory at Jena on 27 May 1943 – both crewmembers, Plt Off R Massie and Sgt G P Lister, were killed. Only three of the eight Mosquitoes despatched by No 105 Sqn bombed the target, whilst three out of six No 139 Sqn aircraft attacked the Schott Glass Works as part of the same raid (*RAF Marham*)

Wg Cdr Reg W Reynolds DSO*, DFC
rests his bandaged hand on the
damaged port engine propeller
blade (both were hit when flak
struck the airscrew) of DZ601 *B-Beer*
whilst posing for the camera with
his navigator, Flt Lt Ted Sismore
DSO, DFC soon after returning from
the attack on the Schott Glass
Works at Jena. This operation was
the last big No 2 Group raid carried
out in daylight by Nos 105 and 139
Sqns (*via Philip Birtles*)

Photographed in the operations
room at Marham just hours after
returning from the Jena raid are Flt
Sgt Leigh Howard (left), who flew as
the cameraman in DZ414/O-Orange,
his pilot, Flt Lt Charles Patterson
(centre), and Wg Cdr Reynolds, who
is enjoying a mug of rum from the
jar after a particularly harrowing
return flight. The latter's left arm is
bandaged as a result of the wounds
sustained in the Jena raid (see
above caption), Reynolds' injuries
having initially been dressed in
flight by his navigator, Ted Sismore
(*Charles Patterson*)

planners back at Marham, and made straight for my beloved Zuider Zee. I turned north and went up to the Causeway, then out between Vlieland and Ameland, where there would be no flak.

'The return was in fact quite traumatic. After landing, I discovered that the target had been attacked, and that one or two Mosquitoes were coming back badly shot up – the flak over the target was worse than I'd thought. Both formations had hit the target without me, so I thought that I'd put up a rather a bad show. They had attacked in deplorable visibility, flying through a balloon barrage over the factory itself. Wg Cdr Reynolds got back, but his aircraft was badly shot up and he had been wounded. His navigator had bound up his injuries, and they'd had to fly back on one engine, plus had got lost. They had flown over some heavily defended areas and been hit again, and Reynolds only just got the aircraft back. He came into the crewroom looking rather washed out and with his arm nestled in a sling.

'The factory had been hit, but just how much damage had been done we didn't know. We had lost five out of fourteen aircraft, so the reaction to the raid was mixed. It was regarded as a tremendous tactical achievement, but the casualties had been worse than expected. After the Jena raid, No 2 Group was kept in Bomber Command (Nos 105 and 139 Sqns were now transferred to No 8 Pathfinder Group for a complete change of role), whilst the rest joined Grp Capt Basil Embry as part of the Tactical Air Force. The Mosquitoes were put onto night bombing, a role which had caught Harris' imagination during our first Berlin trip.'

THE PATHFINDERS

In No 8 Group (PFF), No 105 Sqn would operate alongside No 109 Sqn as the second *Oboe* (a high-level blind bombing radar aid) marker unit, while No 139 Sqn became the 'supporting squadron', going in with the markers themselves. These three units formed the backbone of Air Commodore (later AVM) Donald C T Bennett's specialist Pathfinder Force, which had been formed in August 1942, and increased in size until it achieved group status on 13 January 1943. The PFF markers' job was to 'illuminate' and 'mark' targets with coloured TI's (target indicators) for both the Main Force of 'heavies' and other No 8 Group Mosquitoes. No 109 Sqn had joined No 8 Group at Wyton on 1 June 1942, and *Oboe* had first been used on 20/21 December 1942 when then OC, Sqn Ldr H E 'Hal' Bufton, and his navigator, Flt Lt E L Ifould (along with two other crews), bombed a power-station in Holland.

On 31 December 1942/1 January 1943, sky-marking using *Oboe* was tried for the first time when two Mosquitoes of No 109 Sqn provided the TIs for eight Lancasters of the Pathfinder Force sent to bomb Düsseldorf. Sky markers were parachute flares deployed to pick a spot in the sky in the

An ex-Imperial Airways and Atlantic ferry pilot, Australian AVM Donald C T Bennett (centre), C-in-C No 8 Group (PFF), is seen here with his staff officers at a briefing session. Formed originally from No 3 Group using volunteer crews, No 8 Group started life as a specialist PFF force on 15 August 1942, before achieving fully-fledged group status on 13 January 1943. By March 1945 No 8 Group controlled some 19 squadrons, 10 of which were equipped with Mosquitoes (*via Tom Cushing*)

A fitter carries out work on the starboard engine of DK300, a Mosquito B Mk IV Series II which had been delivered to No 109 Sqn at Stradishall, in Suffolk, on 21 July 1942 to have *Oboe* radar equipment installed. The following month No 109 Sqn moved to Wyton, where DK300 (and eight other B Mk IVs) was used for *Oboe* trials. Although this aircraft survived a lengthy combat tour, it broke up in flight over Pidley, which was then in Huntingdonshire (now Cambridgeshire), on 22 July 1944 whilst serving with No 1655 MTU (*via GMS*)

event of cloud cover over the target area. That same night two *Oboe* Mosquitoes dropped HE bombs through cloud from a height of 28,000 ft onto the nightfighter control room at Florennes airfield, in Belgium.

Oboe was the most accurate form of blind bombing used in World War 2, and it took its name from a radar pulse which sounded like a musical instrument. John C Sampson, a navigator in No 105 Sqn from the summer of 1944 to the end of the war, describes the system employed;

'The radar pulses operated on the range from two ground stations ("Cat" and "Mouse") in England across to the target (following the Normandy invasion, ground stations were located on the continent, thus increasing the effective range of the system). The signals went "line of sight", and did not follow the curvature of the earth, so the further the target, the higher one needed to be. The time on the bombing run was ten minutes on a slightly curved track, as it was a system based on range. The track to the target was extended backwards for a further five minutes. This was known as the "waiting point", but one did not actually wait there – it meant waiting for one's call-in signal. So, at zero minus 15 minutes, one turned onto the track to the target and switched on the *Oboe* receiver and listened out. When one heard the call-in signal we switched on the *Oboe* transmitter and began to receive signals from the ground station.

'The signals were heard by both pilot and navigator, and were used to track the aircraft over the target, If inside the correct line, dots were heard, and if outside the line, dashes, whilst a steady note indicated the target was on track. This signal was heard only by the navigator. When the release signal, which consisted of five dots and a two-second dash, was heard, the navigator released the markers or bombs.'

No 105 Sqn had flown its first *Oboe* operation on 13 July 1943 when

No 109 Sqn's Flt Lt Frank Griggs DFC, RAAF and Flt Lt A P 'Pat' O'Hara DFC*, DFM pose for the camera in front of their distinctively marked B Mk IV Mosquito at RAF Marham in 1943. This crew flew *Oboe* operations until January 1944 when Griggs was repatriated to Australia, O'Hara finishing his second tour (he and Griggs had earlier flown Stirlings together) flying with various pilots including Wg Cdr Peter Kleboe, OC 'A' Flight. On 25 October 1944, whilst marking Essen with red TIs, Kleboe and O'Hara's Mosquito was hit by a piece of flak that came through the windscreen of the aircraft just as the latter lent forward and pressed the lever to open the bomb bay doors. The scorching hot metal tore the left epaulette off O'Hara's battledress and peppered Kleboe's face with fragments of perspex, which left him practically blind. Despite his drastically reduced vision, the pilot got the Mosquito back to Little Staughton and landed it safely. Kleboe was later killed on the Shellhaus raid, flown on 21 March 1945 (*Pat O'Hara*)

Yet another No 109 Sqn B Mk IV Series II to carry nose art, DK333 became one of the first Mosquitoes to drop ground target indicators (250 lb marker bombs) when it participated in a raid on 27 January 1943. This aircraft also served with No 192 Sqn, before finally being struck off charge on 30 May 1945 (*via Phil Jarrett*)

two B Mk IVs attempted to mark Cologne. In September the squadron began precision bombing of pin-point targets in western Germany.

The *Oboe* markers achieved such proficiency that Bennett was able to expand his Mosquito force, and in early 1943 No 8 Group began 'nuisance' raiding. By the summer this had become so effective that the Mosquitoes were now referred to as the Light Night Striking Force (LNSF, or, at Bennett's insistence, the *Fast* Night Striking Force). One of their greatest achievements came during the nine-day long (between 24/25 July and 2 August 1943) Operation *Gomorrah* (the 'Battle of Hamburg') – the PFF and LNSF flew 472 sorties for the loss of just 13 Mosquitoes. The first raid, which was led by both H$_2$S PFF aircraft and standard Mosquitoes, saw TIs used to mark targets for 728 bombers, which dropped 2284 tons of HE and incendiaries onto Hamburg in just 50 minutes, creating a fire-storm which rose to a height of 2 miles.

RAF losses were light due mainly to *Window*, which was being used for the first time – *Window* was the code-name for strips of black paper with aluminium foil stuck to one side, and cut to a length (30 cm by 1.5 cm) equivalent to half the wavelength of the Würzburg ground and *Lichtenstein* air intercept radars. When dropped by aircraft in bundles of 1000 at a time at one-minute intervals, *Window* reflected the radar waves and 'snowed' the tubes.

On 18/19 November 1943, 'spoof' raiding was first tried by No 139 Sqn, who used *Window* to give the impression that they were a large bomber force when in fact they were flying in just squadron strength – whilst this was occurring, the 'heavies' were en route to the real target. On 26 November three Mosquitoes from this unit flew ahead of the Main Force scattering *Window* on the approaches to Berlin, before returning to drop bombs. They also made feint attacks on other targets at distances of up to 50 miles away from the main stream in order to attract nightfighters away from the 'heavies'.

Late in November 1943 No 627 Sqn was formed at Oakington, near Cambridge, followed by No 692 Sqn, which became the fifth Mosquito unit within No 8 Group, at Gravely on 1 January 1944. The latter squadron had the dubious honour of being the first Mosquito unit to drop a 4000-lb bomb (known variously as a 'Blockbuster', 'Cookie' or 'Dangerous Dustbin' because of its shape) on a German target when DZ647 – one of a small number of modified B Mk IVs – released one during a raid on Düsseldorf on 23/24 February. Although the B Mk IV had a strengthened bomb bay and modified bomb bay doors, it was not entirely suitable for the job of carrying a 4000 'pounder'. Nevertheless, 'Cookies' continued to be carried in modified B Mk IVs until the B Mk XVI high-altitude Mosquito (with its bulged bomb bay and more powerful 1680 hp Merlin 72/76, or two 1710-hp 73/77 engines, which gave the aircraft a top speed of 419 mph at 28,500 ft) became operational. No 692 Sqn debuted the B Mk XVI over Duisburg on 5/6 March 1944.

The winter of 1943-44 saw the start of Bomber Command's offensive against Berlin, masterminded by its C-in-C, Air Marshal Harris. Sixteen major raids were flown against the 'Big City' in quick succession, but the capital was too vast, and the weather often too bad, to allow effective results to be achieved. On 1/2 February 1944, No 139 Sqn, which had pioneered the use of Canadian-built Mosquitoes, and was now operating a mix of B Mk IVs, IXs, XVIs and XXs, used H_2S for the first time to mark the target during a raid on Berlin. H_2S provided a map-like image on a CRT (radar scope screen) which, in the Mosquito, was connected to a revolving scanner antennae housed in a bulbous nose radome. Targets had to be carefully selected using H_2S, with city areas sited on coastlines or estuaries being more easily picked out than land-locked targets because of the verifiable distinction between water and land on radar screens.

From 1944, H_2S-equipped B Mk IXs of No 139 Sqn frequently led operations or marked for other Mosquitoes, whilst *Oboe* Mk II-equipped B Mk IXs of Nos 109 and 105 Sqns spearheaded the main force bombing

A train of 4000-lb 'Cookie' bombs arrive at dispersal at Graveley for loading aboard B Mk XXVIs of No 692 Sqn. This unit was formed with B Mk IVs at the Cambridgeshire airfield on 1 January 1944, and flew its first LNSF operation on 1/2 February when three Mosquitoes were sent to bomb Berlin. By early 1944 suitably modified B Mk IVs were capable – just – of carrying a 4000-lb 'Blockbuster', although the outsized weapon had to be carefully 'squeezed' into the strengthened bomb bay, which also boasted redesigned bomb doors. No 692 Sqn had the distinction of being the first Mosquito unit to drop a 4000-lb bomb on Germany when DZ647 (a modified B Mk IV) took part in the Düsseldorf raid on the night of 23/24 February 1944. B Mk XVIs eventually replaced the modified B Mk IVs from June 1944 onwards, the former remaining in service until October 1945 (*via Tom Cushing*)

As with the modified B Mk IV, No 692 Sqn also debuted the first 4000-lb bomb capable B Mk XVIs in combat when a small number participated in a raid on Duisburg on 5/6 March 1944 – 'Cookies' were dropped for the first time on Berlin on 13/14 April, again by No 692 Sqn. The B Mk XVI, with its bulged bomb bay and more powerful Merlin engines, was a much more acceptable 'Cookie carrier' than the 'interim' B Mk IV. This evocative photo shows B Mk XVI MM230 closing on the camera-ship at high altitude. This Mosquito, which had originally been built as a PR IX in November 1943, was retained by de Havilland for development work until struck of charge on 22 October 1946 (*BAe via GMS*)

raids. In the 12 months from January to December 1944, apart from No 692 Sqn, which was mentioned earlier in this chapter, five more Mosquito units joined No 8 Group. The first of these was No 571 Sqn, which formed at Downham Market on 7 April. A shortage of Mosquitoes initially meant that the unit had to operate at half-strength for a time. Although light on aircraft, the unit nevertheless participated in its first mission on the night of 13/14 April, when two crews from No 571 Sqn joined forces with six from No 692 Sqn in an attack on Berlin – each aircraft carried two 50-gallon drop tanks and a 4000-lb bomb.

On 1 August No 608 Sqn formed at Downham Market, and on 15 September No 128 Sqn stood up at Wyton and immediately joined the LNSF. On 25 October No 142 Sqn re-formed at Gransden Lodge, and that same night they flew their first operation when their only two B Mk XXVs were despatched to Cologne. On 18 December No 162 Sqn re-formed at Bourn with B Mk XXVs, and soon accompanied the veteran No 139 Sqn on target-marking duties – No 163 Sqn, the 11th, and final, Mosquito unit within No 8 Group, reformed at Wyton on 25 January 1945 on B Mk XXVs. Led by Wg Cdr (later Air Marshal) Ivor Broom DFC, the squadron flew its first LNSF operation just four days later when four Mosquitoes dropped *Window* at Mainz ahead of the PFF force.

Since the beginning of 1944, No 617 Sqn of 'Dam Buster' fame (led by Wg Cdr Leonard Cheshire VC, DSO*, DFC) had successfully employed the tactic of marking and destroying small industrial targets at night using flares dropped by a Lancaster in a shallow dive at low level. Obviously the Avro 'heavy' had limitations in this role, so Air Marshal the Hon Ralph Cochrane, urged on by Cheshire, gave the unit a Mosquito. No 617 Sqn's first sortie with the type occurred on 5/6 April 1944 when Wg Cdr Cheshire (along with navigator Flg Off Pat Kelly) marked an aircraft factory at Toulouse on his third pass with two red spot flares from a height of 800-1000 ft. He later used this aircraft (ML976/N) on 10/11 April to mark a signals depot at St Cyr during a dive from 5000 to 1000 ft.

These successes led to No 617 Sqn receiving four FB Mk VIs/XVIs, which were first used for marking the Paris-Juvisy marshalling yards on 18/19 April, along with three *Oboe* Mosquitoes of No 8 Group. A force comprising 202 Lancasters from No 5 Group (led by Cheshire himself) and a handful of Mosquitoes carried out a massed attack on the yards. The target area had been marked at each end with red spot-fires, and the Lancasters duly dropped their bombs between the TIs. As a result of the bombing being concentrated, the yards were put out of action and few French lives were lost – all but one Lancaster returned safely to base. Indeed, the railway yards were so badly damaged that they were only reopened in 1947. La Chapelle was marked on 20/21 April by three No 617 Sqn Mosquitoes, whilst Brunswick became the first German city to be targeted by the low level marking method on 22/23 April.

Sir Arthur Harris, who had sanctioned the release of the four Mosquitoes, said they could be retained by No 617 Sqn if Munich was hit heavily on the night of 24/25 April – in preparation for this long range operation, the quartet of aircraft moved to Manston, on the Kent coast. Once over the target the four Mosquitoes proved highly successful in completing their task, Cheshire diving from 12,000 to 3000 ft and then flying repeatedly over the city at little more than 700 ft, coming under fire for a whole 12 minutes before leaving the area. Sqn Ldr Dave Shannon dived from 15,000 to 4000 ft, but his markers hung up, whilst the fourth Mosquito got four spot flares away. Ninety per cent of the bombs fell in the right place, doing more damage in one night than had been achieved by Bomber Command and the Eighth Air Force combined in the preceding four years. Cheshire's contribution to the success of the raid was mentioned in his VC citation, issued on 8 September 1944.

In April 1944 No 627 Sqn was transferred from No 8 to No 5 Group at Woodhall Spa for specialised marking operations. The Lancaster pathfinder squadrons would identify the target areas on H_2S and then lay a concentrated carpet of flares, under which No 627 Sqn would locate and mark the precise aiming point in a shallow dive with 500-lb spot-fires. Under the direction of a 'Master of Ceremonies' in one of the pathfinder Lancasters, the target would then be destroyed by No 5 Group

Left and below
A 'Cookie' is slowly winched into the bulged bomb bay of a No 692 Sqn Mosquito in preparation for a raid on the 'Big City'. This aircraft was subsequently flown to Berlin by Canadians Flt Lts Andy Lockhart and Ralph Wood (navigator) – the pair completed 50 operations in Mosquitoes, including 18 trips to Berlin (*Mrs Phyllis Wood*)

Their 50-gallon underwing drop tanks clearly visible, a trio of No 128 Sqn B Mk XVIs taxy onto the runway at Wyton at the start of yet another sortie to Berlin. Mosquitoes flew so often to the 'Big City' that crews dubbed the mission the 'Berlin Express', with the different routes there and back being known as 'platforms one, two and three'. No 128 Sqn, which reformed as a Pathfinder unit within No 8 (PFF) Group on 15 September 1944, was initially issued with B Mk XXs before standardising on the B Mk XVI (*via Jerry Scutts*)

Already a veteran of an operational tour with No 692 Sqn, B Mk IV (Modified) DZ633 went on to see more action with No 627 Sqn following its arrival at Woodhall Spa on 12 August 1944. Just 19 days later the bomber was hit by flak over Rollencourt, and despite suffering considerable damage to both wings, its crew managed to reach Woodhall Spa. Having been repaired, DZ633 was struck again by flak on 17 September over the Boulogne area during a photo recce mission – one engine was hit and had to be feathered, but again the aircraft made it back to base. On 31 December 1944 DZ633 took part in the raid on the Gestapo HQ at Oslo and was duly hit again by a cannon shell over the target. Flt Lt Wallace 'Johnno' S Gaunt DFC* was struck by shell splinters in the thigh, and his pilot, Flt Lt Peter F Mallender DFC, gave him first aid prior to performing a ground loop landing at Peterhead. The aircraft was repaired for a third time and returned to operations on 12 February 1945 – it was finally struck off charge on 30 May 1945 (*Andy Thomas*)

heavy bombers. This group was now used exclusively in support of the bombing campaign against interdiction targets for Operation *Overlord*, as Flt L J R 'Benny' Goodman, a pilot with No 627 Sqn, recalls;

'The Americans were nervous about the gun battery at St Martin de Varreville, behind *Utah* beach. This presented a threat to Allied shipping approaching Normandy, and also to the troops landing on *Utah* beach. It was decided that No 5 Group would attack this precision target, so on the night of 28/29 May 1944, a force of 64 Lancasters, led by a flare force from Nos 83 and 97 Lancaster Pathfinder Sqns, and four Mosquitoes of No 627 Sqn, flew to St Martin de Varreville. The flare force identified the gun battery on their H$_2$S sets and laid a carpet of flares over the target. At Zero Hour minus five minutes, the Mosquitoes roared in at 2000 ft and identified the gun battery visually. The first pilot to see the target called "Tally Ho" on his VHF radio to warn his companions to keep out of the way, and then proceeded to dive at the gun, releasing red TIs at the appropriate point in the dive. His companions followed suit, making individual dives on the battery and creating a box of red TIs around it. The Master Bomber now called in the Main Force, with each aircraft carrying several 1000-lb armour-piercing bombs, and the target was obliterated.

'An American parachute force landed near St Martin de Varreville on D-Day, and an element of the 502nd Regiment made for the coastal battery. Their orders were to overrun the battery and to crush the garrison if necessary. Capt Frank Lilleyman, the first US soldier to land in Normandy on D-Day, reconnoitered the battery and discovered that it had

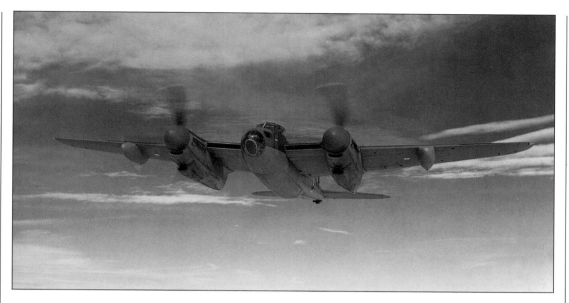

A true combat veteran, B Mk XVI ML963 is seen wearing the markings of No 571 Sqn. Prior to being issued to this unit (who used it on their very first sortie on 12/13 April 1944 – a raid to Osnabruck), the bomber had seen service with Nos 109 and 692 Sqns. This classic Charles E Brown photo, taken during a test flight from Hatfield on 30 September 1944, shows the Mosquito immediately after major repair work had been carried out by the manufacturers to rectify severe flak damage sustained by the aircraft during an operation to Scholven on 6 July 1944 – its crew on this raid was Wt Off Russell Longworth and Plt Off Ken Davidson. This was the second time that ML963 had suffered combat damage, having earlier been hit by flak during a raid on Brunsbuttellkoog on 12 May – on this occasion repairs had commenced on 25 May and the aircraft returned to the squadron on 26 June. ML963 was reissued to No 571 Sqn for a second time on 18 October 1944, and on New Year's Day 1945 it was used by Flt Lt N J Griffiths and Flg Off W R Ball in the precision raids on railway tunnels in the Eiffel region during the Battle of the Bulge – their 4,000-lb delayed-action bomb destroyed a tunnel at Bitburg. ML963 was lost during a raid on Berlin on 10/11 April 1945 following an engine fire, its crew, Flg Off Richard Oliver and Flt Sgt Max Young, successfully bailing out near the Elbe

been bombed out and abandoned as a result of the No 5 Group attack.'

Post-D-Day, No 5 Group Mosquitoes continued their marking of targets in France for the Main Force, while Bennett's LNSF in No 8 Group went after German cities. Canadians Flt Lts Andy Lockhart and Ralph Wood (the former's navigator) flew 50 operations in Mosquitoes with No 692 Sqn during this time and into 1945. Wood recalls that the 'daddy of them all' occurred on the night of 5/6 October 1944 when six Mosquitoes from No 692 Sqn (five carried a 1000-lb mine and one a 1500-lb mine) and four from No 571 Sqn mined the Kiel Canal;

'We dropped our "vegetable" from a height of 100 ft. It was "wizard" flying at roof-top level over the villages and farm houses. The Canal was well defended by 97 light AA guns, balloons and 25 searchlights. One searchlight got us and a gun opened fire at our Mosquito from head-on when we were about 200 ft off the deck. It was rather alarming, but the gunners missed us. All of the Mosquitoes got back, although one pilot flew back with a dead navigator beside him for company. We really enjoyed ourselves, but we had the "twitch" before reaching the target.'

On 6/7 November, Bomber Command despatched 235 Lancasters to attack the Mittelland Canal at Gravenhorst – the target marking was carried out by seven Mosquitoes from No 627 Sqn. The latter eventually found the canal after great difficulty, whereupon Sqn Ldr F W Boyle, RAAF and Flt Lt L C E De Vigne dropped their marker with such a degree of accuracy that it fell into the water and was extinguished! Only 31 Lancasters bombed before the Master Bomber called for the raid to be abandoned. The 48 Mosquitoes despatched to Gelsenkirchen on a 'spoof' raid to draw German nightfighters away from both the Mittleland attack and a No 3 Group raid on Koblenz had better luck.

The Gelsenkirchen raid began as planned some five minutes ahead of the two main attacks at 19.25 hours. The city was still burning as a result of the afternoon raid by 738 RAF 'heavies', and from 25,000 ft, the Mosquitoes added their red and green TIs and HE to the fires. A few searchlights and only very light flak greeted the crews over the devastated city.

Berlin was the most frequent target city for the LNSF. The Mosquitoes flew there so often (170 times, 36 of these on consecutive nights) that the raids were called the 'milk run' or, alternatively, the 'Berlin Express', and the different routes there and back were known as 'Platforms one, two and three'. A usual bomb load was 4000 lbs, and a typical trip to the 'snake's home' would see feint attacks made on a couple of cities enroute to the target, before *Window* was used to disrupt the enemy's radar nearer to Berlin itself. Flt Lts Andy Lockhart and Ralph Wood flew 18 operations to Berlin, the former recalling;

B Mk XVI '8K-R' of No 571 Sqn was flown from Oakington in 1944 by Flg Off H A 'Mike' Hooper DFC and Flt Sgt Alex Arbuckle DFM. Both men survived their tour (May to November 1944) and were duly posted to No 1655 MTU (*Barry Blunt via Andy Thomas*)

'Once over Berlin we were usually caught in a huge cone of searchlights that so blinded Andy that he couldn't read the instruments – "Are we upside down or not?" he'd ask. I'd look down at the bombs exploding below and assure him that we were rightside up! As the anti-aircraft crap seemed to surround us, Andy would throw our *Moncton Express* around the skies, trying to get out of the searchlights. On three occasions we lost an engine about now and had to limp home, one set of searchlights passing us on to another set, and so on, until they ran out of lights.

'Sometimes the boys were coned here and there, but no flak was shot up the beams, which indicated that enemy fighters were present. When over the target, we'd bomb and get out as fast as we could. This is when I'd sit

Another evocative Charles E Brown photograph of No 571 Sqn's ML963 – coded 'K-King' – taken on 30 September 1944 over Hatfield

in my seat, the blood draining out of my face and my stomach in tight knots. "Jesus, this could be it", I thought. And after tight moments like this I'd say, "Andy. Pass the beads". Once we dropped our wing tanks along with the "cookie" as the groundcrew had it wired up wrong. We were coned over the "Big City" but got out of it in four minutes, with only one hunk of flak in our wing. I hope my 18 visits to Berlin accomplished something. On our return trips we faced the terrors of flak and a new adversary in the form of the first jets rising into the skies over Germany.'

Plt Off J F P Archbold, navigator to Plt Off R H M 'Percy' Vere of No 692 Sqn, described his 'Big City Bash' to Berlin in MM224/'K-King' on 31 December 1944 (their 27th operation) in the following terms;

'Began *Windowing*, eight minutes to go. The chute is on the floor between your feet – you have to bend almost double to drop the bundles. You can hear a crackle on the R/T as they open up in the slipstream. Back-breaking job this – makes you sweat like blazes. Five minutes to go – should see the first TI soon. There goes the last *Window* bundle – I stretch up and look out. Still over 10/10ths cloud. Good. There's the first TI over to port. I dive into the bombing position – "dive" is a misnomer. With all the kit I've got on it's more like a wrestling match! I switch on the sighting head and put the final wind velocity on the computer box, then wait for the TIs to come into view. The nose is frosted up except for the optically-flat, heated, bombing window, so I can't see very far ahead.

'A couple of minutes to go now. "More TIs down – reds and greens", says Ron. "Bomb doors open". "Bomb doors open", I repeat, and hear the rumbling roar as they open and the wind whistles into the bomb bay. "I'm running on a bunch of three", says Ron. "Can you see them yet?" I crane my neck close to the window and look ahead sideways. "Yep. I can just see

A 4000 'pounder' bearing the festive inscription 'Happy Xmas Adolf' is wheeled into position for hoisting aboard B Mk XVI MM199 'Q-Queenie' of No 128 Sqn at Wyton in late 1944 – this 'Cookie carrier' was regularly flown by Flg Offs B D McEwan DFC and Harbottle. On 28/29 August 1944, McEwan returned from a raid on Essen with his 4000-lb bomb still aboard. MM199, which had previously served with No 105 Sqn prior to being issued to No 128 Sqn, failed to return from a mission to Hannover on 5 February 1945 (*via Jerry Scutts*)

B Mk IX LR503 set a Bomber Command record for the Mosquito by completing 213 operational sorties (the aircraft flew firstly with No 109 Sqn, before being passed onto No 105 Sqn) between 1943-45. This photo, taken at Bourn, in Cambridgeshire, soon after the bomber had returned from its 203rd mission, shows the aircrew watching the aircraft's scoreboard being brought up to date (*via Phil Jarrett*)

By the spring of 1945 Bomber Command HQ had decided that LR503 had earned a break from the frontline, so Flt Lt Maurice Briggs DSO, DFC, DFM (right) and navigator Flg Off John Baker DFC* (themselves veterans of 107 sorties) flew the Mosquito to Canada for a goodwill tour. As can be seen from this shot, taken on 23 April 1945, the bomber's white dope bomb tally was resprayed in a darker shade following the fitment of a new glazed nose fairing – note that Hitler's uniform, the bomb above his head and the tail of the wasp also appear to have been touched up in a darker colour. Both Briggs and Baker were killed when LR503 inexplicably crashed at Calgary Airport during a flying display on 10 May 1945 (*via Jerry Scutts*)

them. OK now, left-left, left-left, steady – we're running up nicely. Keep weaving a bit. We've a minute or so to go yet". I get the TIs up on the centreline of the graticule and thumb the release switch. I will press this when the markers reach the cross line.

'A couple of big white flashes under the cloud up ahead show that the first two "Cookies" have gone down. I notice them almost subconsciously. "A little bit of flak to starboard", says Ron. "OK. Keep going", I reply. "Right, right a little – steady now, steady. . . BOMB GONE!", as I press the tit. There's a thud underneath as the lug springs back and releases the bomb. The camera whirs and the red light on the selector box comes on. We have to keep straight and level for 45 seconds to get the photo of our bomb burst in relation to the TIs so as to be able to plot the accuracy later on. I scramble back into my seat and look down the window chute. The wait seems endless. "Bomb doors closed", says Ron. The camera green light comes on. "Hold it", I say. There is a tremendous flash under the cloud. "There she goes. OK. Let's get the hell out of here", and we turn south-west to get out of the target area.'

At first light on the morning after this mission (New Year's Day 1945), with the Battle of the Bulge still raging in the Ardennes, No 8 Group Mosquitoes were asked to fly one of the most remarkable daylight operations of the war. Bomber Command had to cut the railway supply lines through the Eifel region between the Rhine and the Ardennes, so while the 'heavies' bombed marshalling yards near Koblenz and Cologne, precision attacks on 14 railway tunnels in the target area were carried out by 17

Flt Lt Ed Boulter, and his navigator Sgt Chris Hart DFM, pose in front of KB403 'B-Bertie', a Canadian-built B Mk XXV (Merlin 225 powered) of No 163 Sqn, at Wyton in early 1945. Reformed on 25 January 1945 and predominantly staffed by ex-No 128 Sqn personnel (and aircraft) under the command of Wg Cdr Ivor Broom DFC, the unit flew their first LNSF operation on the night of 28/29 January – four B Mk XXVs dropped *Window* at Mainz ahead of the PFF force. 'B-Bertie' was flown by Boulter and Hart on 17 LNSF operations (*Ed Boulter Collection*)

Mosquitoes of Nos 128, 571 and 692 Sqns. Each aircraft carried a 4000-lb delayed-action bomb, which the crew skip-bombed into the mouths of the tunnels from a height of between 100 and 200 ft. PF411 (a No 128 Sqn B Mk XVI) crashed on take-off, killing the crew, whilst the remaining four Mosquitoes from this unit enjoyed mixed results. Six out of seven B Mk XVIs of No 692 Sqn bombed tunnels near Mayen, losing PF414 (and crewmen Flt Lt George Nairn and Sgt Danny Lunn) to light flak. It was left to the five crews from No 571 Sqn to cause the most damage, with one bomb dropped by B Mk XVI ML963/'K-King' (crewed by Flt Lt Norman J Griffiths and Flg Off W R Ball) destroying a tunnel at Bitburg.

With the war in Europe reaching a conclusion, the Mosquitoes were repeatedly called upon to mark for the bombers in daylight. One of the most dramatic marking operations of the war occurred on 14 March when a Mosquito from No 5 Group and eight *Oboe* Mosquitoes of Nos 105 and 109 Sqns set out to mark the Bielefeld and Arnsburg viaducts for

B Mk XVI MM188/'N-Nan' of No 692 Sqn provides the backdrop for Plt Offs J F P Archbold (left), navigator, and R H M 'Percy' Vere (right), who used this aircraft on three sorties – to Berlin on 23/24 October 1944, Stuttgart on 5/6 November 1944 and Berlin again on 5/6 March 1945. Each time the aircraft's warload comprised a single 4000-lb bomb (*Sqn Ldr John Archbold*)

fellow group Lancasters. Although the four Mosquitoes attempting to mark the latter target for No 9 Sqn failed in the attempt (resulting in no damage being caused to the viaduct) and three of the *Oboe* Mosquitoes were unable to mark the Bielefeld viaduct for No 617 Sqn, Flg Off G W Edwards of No 105 Sqn (in B Mk XVI MM191) succeeded in getting his markers on target. This resulted in more than 100 yards of the viaduct collapsing under the weight of the explosions – 28 of the 32 Lancasters despatched carried *Tallboys* and one from No 617 Sqn dropped the first 22,000-lb *Grand Slam* bomb.

The biggest No 8 Group Mos-

quito operation to Berlin took place on 21/22 March when 142 aircraft carried out two attacks for the loss of one aircraft. The group made their last daylight raid on 6 March when 48 Mosquitoes, led by *Oboe* leaders from No 109 Sqn, bombed Wesel. The final attack on Berlin by Mosquitoes came on 20/21 April when 76 aircraft completed six raids. On 25 April, 359 Lancasters and 16 Mosquitoes (including eight *Oboe* markers) went to bomb Hitler's 'Eagle's Nest' chalet and SS barracks at Berchtesgaden, but the Alps blocked all radar signals and none of the *Oboe* aircraft were able to bomb.

On 25/26 April 12 Mosquitoes dropped leaflets over PoW camps in Germany telling Allied prisoners that the end of the war was imminent, followed three days later by the commencement of Operation *Manna* – the air-dropping of food to the starving Dutch population in German-occupied Holland. *Oboe* Mosquitoes were extensively employed marking drop zones for RAF and USAAF heavy bombers, whose bomb bays were filled with provisions instead of high explosives

It was feared that Germany might stage a last stand in Norway when troopships assembled at Kiel, so, on the night of 2/3 May, three raids by 142 Mosquitoes from No 8 Group and 37 Mosquitoes of No 100 Group were made. This was Bomber Command's final operation of the war.

During January-May 1945 the LNSF flew almost 4000 sorties, whilst the total war tally for Mosquitoes of No 8 Group stood at 28,215 sorties by VE-Day. Despite this huge number, the Mosquito force suffered the lowest losses in Bomber Command – 108 aircraft, or 1 per 2800 sorties, while 88 more were damaged beyond repair. Well over two-thirds of these sorties were flown on nights when the Main Force was grounded.

B Mk XVI RV297/'M5-F' of No 128 Sqn taxies out at Wyton on the night of 21/22 March 1945. This aircraft was just one of 142 No 8 Group (PFF) Mosquitoes that made two raids on Berlin – only one aircraft was subsequently lost in this operation. LNSF Mosquitos raided Berlin 170 times in total, 36 of these on consecutive nights. RV297 saw service with Nos 692, 128, 139, 572 and 98 Sqn prior to being retired to the RAF's Signalling School on 5 August 1948

Groundcrewmen manhandle a 4000-lb 'Cookie' in the direction of the bomb bay of B Mk XVI PF432 (a No 128 Sqn machine based at Wyton) on 21 March 1945. This aircraft duly participated in one of the two raids staged that night on the 'Big City'. Prior to serving with this unit, PF432 had seen action with No 692 Sqn (*via Jerry Scutts*)

COLOUR PLATES

This ten-page colour section profiles representative Mosquito fighter-bombers from many of the frontline squadrons that saw service with the type within the RAF and RAAF between 1942 and 1945. The colour artwork has been specially-commissioned for this volume, and profile artist Chris Davey (using extensive references supplied by Mike Bailey) and figure artist Mike Chappell have gone to great pains to illustrate the aircraft, and their crews, as accurately as possible following research from original sources. Mosquitoes that have never previously been seen in profile are featured alongside accurate renditions of some of the more familiar aircraft of the period.

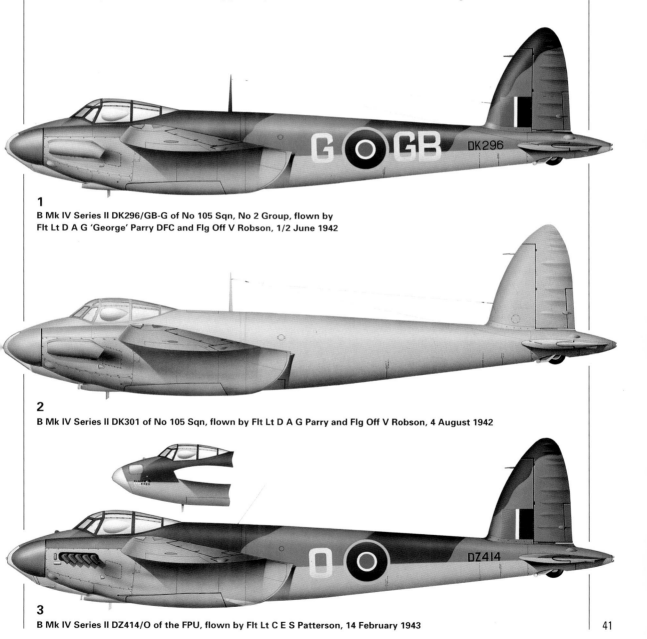

1
B Mk IV Series II DK296/GB-G of No 105 Sqn, No 2 Group, flown by Flt Lt D A G 'George' Parry DFC and Flg Off V Robson, 1/2 June 1942

2
B Mk IV Series II DK301 of No 105 Sqn, flown by Flt Lt D A G Parry and Flg Off V Robson, 4 August 1942

3
B Mk IV Series II DZ414/O of the FPU, flown by Flt Lt C E S Patterson, 14 February 1943

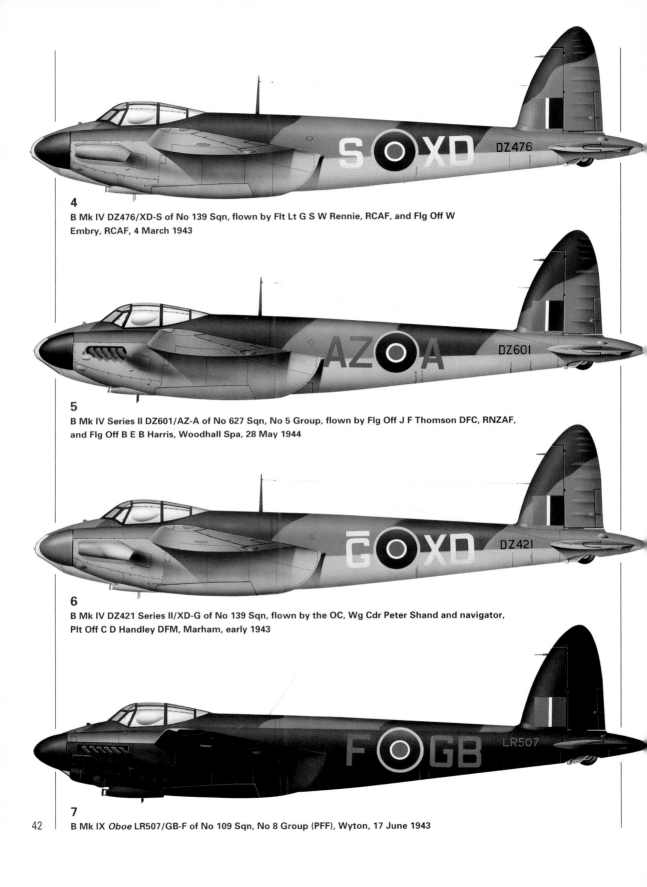

4

B Mk IV DZ476/XD-S of No 139 Sqn, flown by Flt Lt G S W Rennie, RCAF, and Flg Off W
Embry, RCAF, 4 March 1943

5

B Mk IV Series II DZ601/AZ-A of No 627 Sqn, No 5 Group, flown by Flg Off J F Thomson DFC, RNZAF,
and Flg Off B E B Harris, Woodhall Spa, 28 May 1944

6

B Mk IV DZ421 Series II/XD-G of No 139 Sqn, flown by the OC, Wg Cdr Peter Shand and navigator,
Plt Off C D Handley DFM, Marham, early 1943

7

B Mk IX *Oboe* LR507/GB-F of No 109 Sqn, No 8 Group (PFF), Wyton, 17 June 1943

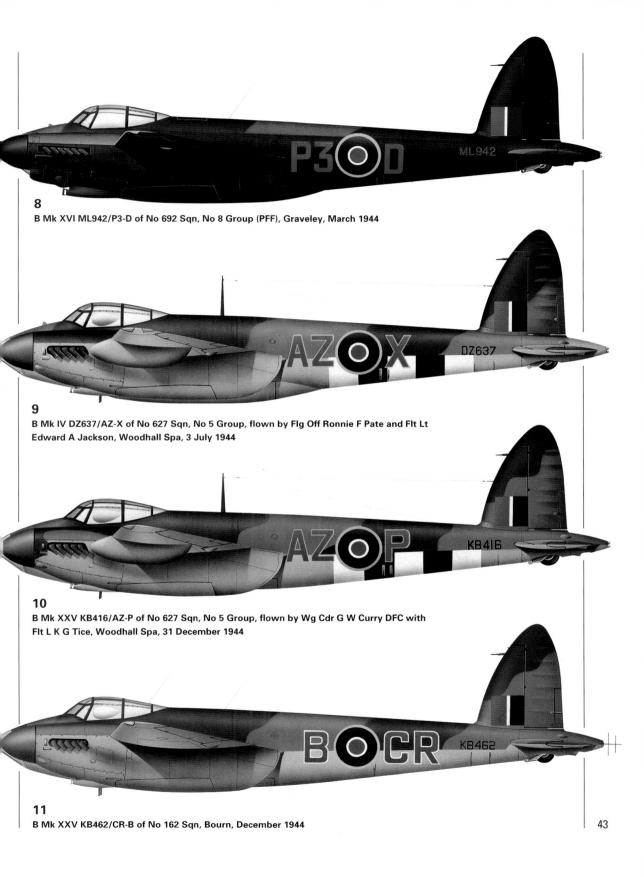

8
B Mk XVI ML942/P3-D of No 692 Sqn, No 8 Group (PFF), Graveley, March 1944

9
B Mk IV DZ637/AZ-X of No 627 Sqn, No 5 Group, flown by Flg Off Ronnie F Pate and Flt Lt
Edward A Jackson, Woodhall Spa, 3 July 1944

10
B Mk XXV KB416/AZ-P of No 627 Sqn, No 5 Group, flown by Wg Cdr G W Curry DFC with
Flt L K G Tice, Woodhall Spa, 31 December 1944

11
B Mk XXV KB462/CR-B of No 162 Sqn, Bourn, December 1944

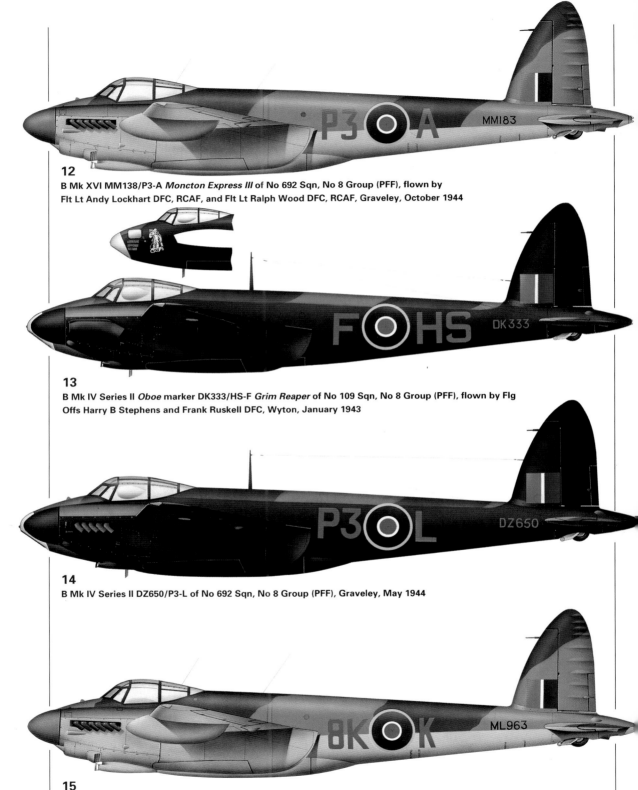

12
B Mk XVI MM138/P3-A *Moncton Express III* of No 692 Sqn, No 8 Group (PFF), flown by
Flt Lt Andy Lockhart DFC, RCAF, and Flt Lt Ralph Wood DFC, RCAF, Graveley, October 1944

13
B Mk IV Series II *Oboe* marker DK333/HS-F *Grim Reaper* of No 109 Sqn, No 8 Group (PFF), flown by Flg
Offs Harry B Stephens and Frank Ruskell DFC, Wyton, January 1943

14
B Mk IV Series II DZ650/P3-L of No 692 Sqn, No 8 Group (PFF), Graveley, May 1944

15
B Mk XVI ML963/8K-K of No 692 Sqn, flown by Flg Off Richard Oliver and Flt Sgt Max Young, April 1945

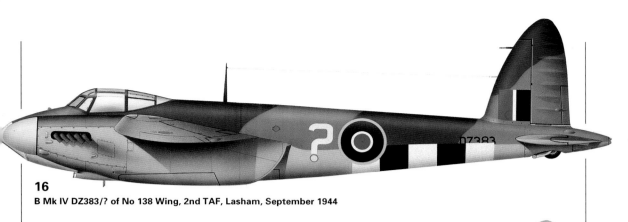

16
B Mk IV DZ383/? of No 138 Wing, 2nd TAF, Lasham, September 1944

17
FB VI MM404/SB-T of No 464 Sqn, RAAF, No 140 Wing, 2nd TAF, flown by Sqn Ldr
Ian McRitchie, RAAF, and Flt Lt R W 'Sammy' Sampson, 18 February 1944

18
FB VI MM417/EG-T of No 487 Sqn, RNZAF, No 140 Wing, No 2 Group, 2nd TAF, late February 1944

19
FB VI MM403/SB-V of No 464 Sqn, RAAF, No 140 Wing, No 2 Group, 2nd TAF, 18 February 1944

20
FB VI HX917/EG-E of No 487 Sqn, RNZAF, Hunsdon, July 1943

21
FB VI LR366/SY-L of No 613 'City of Manchester' Sqn, No 138 Wing, 2nd TAF, Lasham, January 1944

22
FB VI PZ306/YH-Y of No 21 Sqn, No 140 Wing, No 2 Group, 2nd TAF, flown by
Sqn Ldr A F 'Tony' Carlisle DFC and Flt Lt N J 'Rex' Ingram, RNZAF, 21 March 1945

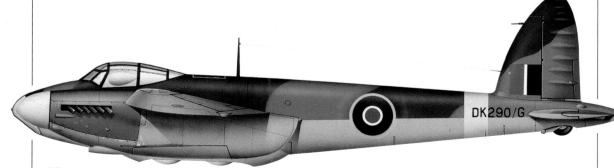

23
B Mk IV Series II DK290/G *Highball* , A&AEE Boscombe Down, April 1943

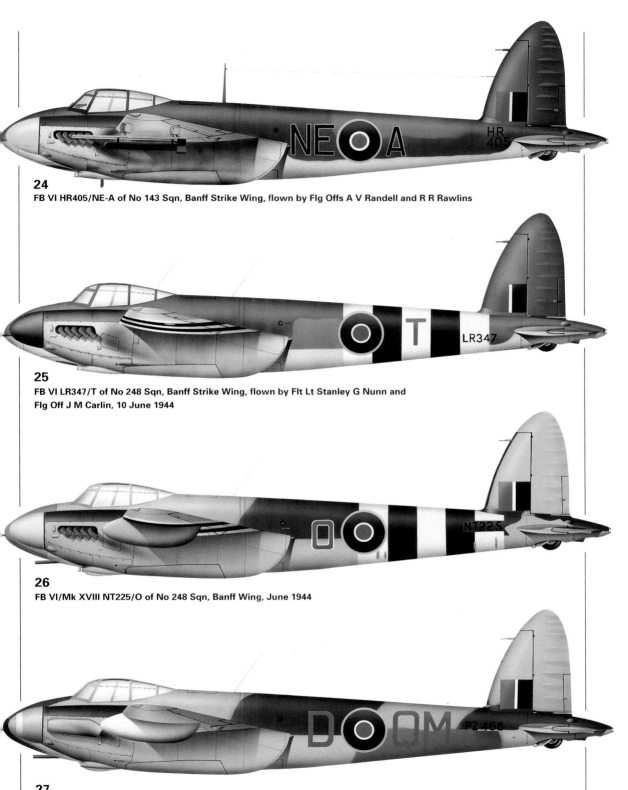

24
FB VI HR405/NE-A of No 143 Sqn, Banff Strike Wing, flown by Flg Offs A V Randell and R R Rawlins

25
FB VI LR347/T of No 248 Sqn, Banff Strike Wing, flown by Flt Lt Stanley G Nunn and
Flg Off J M Carlin, 10 June 1944

26
FB VI/Mk XVIII NT225/O of No 248 Sqn, Banff Wing, June 1944

27
FB XVIII PZ468/QM-D of No 248 Sqn, North Coates, April 1945

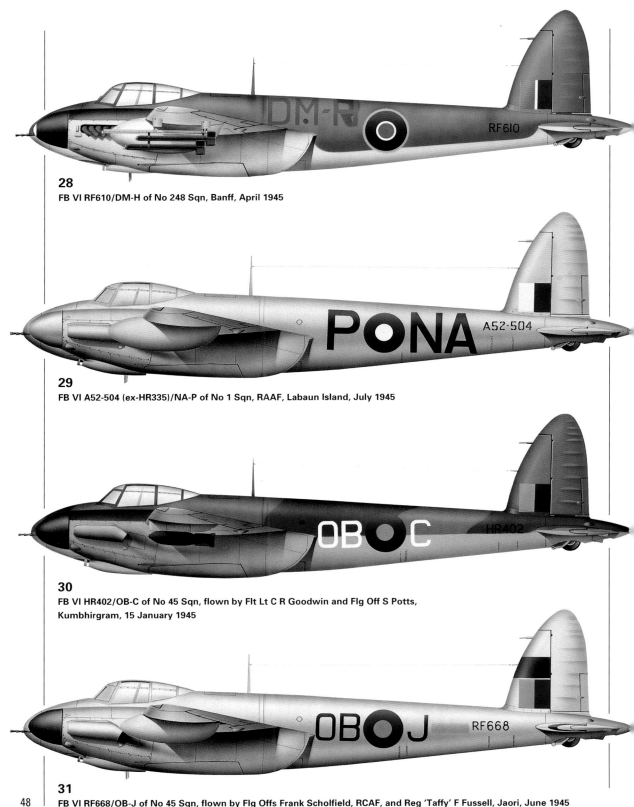

28
FB VI RF610/DM-H of No 248 Sqn, Banff, April 1945

29
FB VI A52-504 (ex-HR335)/NA-P of No 1 Sqn, RAAF, Labaun Island, July 1945

30
FB VI HR402/OB-C of No 45 Sqn, flown by Flt Lt C R Goodwin and Flg Off S Potts, Kumbhirgram, 15 January 1945

31
FB VI RF668/OB-J of No 45 Sqn, flown by Flg Offs Frank Scholfield, RCAF, and Reg 'Taffy' F Fussell, Jaori, June 1945

1
Wg Cdr Hughie Edwards VC, DSO,
DFC, OC No 105 Sqn, Marham,
December 1942

2
Grp Capt Max Aitken DSO, DFC,
OC Banff Strike Wing, Banff, October
1944

3
Wg Cdr John de Lacy Wooldridge DSO,
DFC, DFM, OC No 105 Sqn, Marham,
June 1943

4
Flt Lt R W 'Sammy' Sampson, RAAF, of No 464 Sqn, RAAF, Hunsdon, February 1944

5
Wt Off Davison of No 84 Sqn, Kumbhirgam, Assam, September 1944

6
Grp Capt Percy C Pickard DSO, DFC, attached to No 487 Sqn, RNZAF, Hunsdon, February 1944

2nd TAF

On 1 June 1943, No 2 Group's 11 Norfolk-based Boston, Ventura and Mitchell squadrons were used to form the 2nd Tactical Air Force under the command of AVM Basil Embry. Its brief was simple – help prepare the way for the invasion of the continent, which was planned for the summer of 1944. Embry, whose command immediately began moving to airfields in Hampshire so as to be nearer to the invasion coastline, wanted Mosquito FB VIs, but the 'wooden wonder' was in short supply, so priority was given to the re-equipment of the three units flying Lockheed's obsolescent Ventura – Nos 21, 464 (RAAF) and 487 (RNZAF) Sqns.

Flt Lt Charles Patterson, who at this time was flying the Film Unit's Mosquito B Mk IV DZ414 within the newly-created 2nd TAF, explains;

'The Ventura must have been quite the worst aircraft ever sent into operation. Not only was it extremely limited from an operational standpoint, but it was also an absolute devil to fly, being heavy, cumbersome and unmanoeuvrable. Due to the dynamic drive and determination of Basil Embry, all three Ventura squadrons were re-equipped with Mosquito FB VI fighter-bombers.'

The FB VI was a day and night fighter-bomber, intruder and long range fighter, powered by two 1460 hp Merlin 21/23s or two 1635 hp Merlin 25s. The prototype flew for the first time on 1 June 1942, and production aircraft began rolling out the de Havilland factory in February 1943. Ultimately, some 2289 (almost a third of the total Mosquito production) would be built. Charles Patterson again;

'A conversion flight was formed at Sculthorpe under Sqn Ldr George Parry DSO, DFC*, and I was his deputy. We converted these three-squadrons to Mosquitoes in about six weeks (Nos 464 and 487 Sqns

The Mosquito FB VI was used exclusively by the six fighter-bomber squadrons of Nos 138 and 140 Wings of the 2nd Tactical Air Force. FB VI HX917/EG-E of No 487 Sqn, RNZAF, No 140 Wing, is seen here taxying out at the start of a sortie from its Hunsdon base in July 1943. Mosquito day bombers were camouflaged in dark green/light grey upper surfaces and light grey undersurfaces, with duck egg blue spinners and fuselage band. This scheme was modelled on Fighter Command colours of the same period in an effort to make attacking Luftwaffe fighter pilots believe the FB VIs were actually armed fighter variants of the Mosquito. Sadly, this ruse did not work so well at night, and HX917 was lost on a nocturnal intruder raid over France on 5 July 1944

received their first FB VIs in August, and No 21 Sqn got theirs inSeptember, all three units going on to form No 140 Wing), giving dual all the time until they flew their first operation, which was a comparatively easy one.'

On Sunday, 3 October 1943, every bomber squadron in No 2 Group was allocated one in a series of transformer stations between Paris and Brittany which were to be attacked from low level. Nos 487 and 464 Sqn's targets were the power-stations at Pont Chateau and Mur de Bretange. Patterson continues;

'I was to film the attack by No 487 Sqn. We all went down to Exeter. Basil Embry decided to go on the trip himself and fly somewhere towards the rear of No 464 Sqn. He took his navigator, David Atcherley, who was the twin brother of the famous Wg Cdr D F W 'Batchie' Atcherley of Fighter Command. His SASO (Senior Air Staff Officer) at No 2 Group, Grp Capt Percy Pickard, went too.

'All went smoothly, with the normal low level approach to the coast and then the shallow dive onto the first target. I carried on alone as usual, having to do my own map reading. As I came over the brow of a hill, my second target became clearly visible on my starboard wingtip, and at this point I got over confident – something that I had never previously allowed myself to become, because it usually had fatal results. Having flown past the target and alerted the area to my presence, I did a big sweep round in full view of any gunners and came in and attacked. I noticed that the target was quite undamaged – obviously No 484 Sqn had missed it altogether. I dropped my bombs.

'Then there was a tremendous bang in the cockpit, followed by a near-instantaneous cloud of blue smoke – I had just had my first experience of my aircraft being properly hit in a key area by a 20 mm cannon shell. My immediate reaction was to test the controls, and soon I realised that the aircraft was flying quite normally. We got clear of the target area and I began to feel a bit of a sting in my back – that was all. I was suddenly aware of the red face of the film cameraman (who had been in the nose adjusting his equipment) looking in bewilderment at me through the smoke. I said, "Don't just sit there gawping. Get back into your seat and get your map out and try and find out where we're supposed to be going. What are you looking like that for? The aircraft's perfectly all right".

'He pointed, and I turned round and had a quick look. The whole of the back of the cockpit had gone! A cap of mine which I always left behind my seat was in shreds. The radio and *Gee* set had been smashed too. I had been saved by the armour-plated seat, which had taken the blast, and the sting in my back was the result of a few small bits of shrapnel that had penetrated the plating. We carried on, with a bit of roaring noise from the

This still was taken from the cine camera film shot from Wg Cdr Bob Iredale's No 464 Sqn FB VI MM412/SB-F during Operation *Jericho* – the precision attack on Amiens Prison on 18 February 1944. One of the most famous missions of the war, the raid saw the prison walls breached by 12 FB VIs from Nos 464, RAAF, and 487, RNZAF, Sqns. This action allowed many of the 700 inmates to escape, although most were latter recaptured. The aircraft trailing in MM412's wake is MM402/SB-A, flown by Sqn Ldr W R C Sugden, and his navigator Flg Off A H Bridger. The latter FB VI was lost on operations on 21 March 1944, but MM412 survived a further tour of combat with No 487 Sqn and time with No 13 OTU and No 1 Overseas Ferry Unit, before eventually being sold to the Yugoslav Air Force in April 1952 (*via Jerry Scutts*)

The graphic results of the precision attack on Amiens Prison – both the northern and southern perimeter walls were breached. The attackers came in from the north, so it must be assumed that the southern breach, to the left of the main gate, was caused by a bomb that skidded through the prison after being dropped from the east or the north. Both Plt Off D R Fowler of No 487 Sqn, flying HX974/EG-J, and Sqn Ldr Ian McRitchie of No 464 Sqn, in MM404/SB-T, have since claimed the same hole! (*via GMS*)

wind. Because I was flying a Mosquito B Mk IV, I had enough petrol to head on back to Norfolk, so I had returned to base with the film long before any of the others. My navigator and I went to tea, but we had great difficulty getting served our bacon and eggs because the WAAFs who manned the canteen said we couldn't have been in operations because nobody was back yet. I had to take off my battledress jacket and let the girl inspect the blood on my shirt in order to convince her!

'During these first few weeks after the wing had converted from Venturas to Mosquitoes, there were several botched up and aborted raids due to the fact that none of the experience gained by Nos 105 and 139 Sqns during their splendid months of 1942-43 was available, or used. Many of the losses suffered during those first weeks could have been completely avoided. They made all the same mistakes that we had done two years before.

'One more trip took place to try and rectify these problems. No 487 Sqn was sent out under a wing commander to do a low level daylight attack on an oil refinery on the River Loire, near St Nazaire. I would hopefully bring back film of an oil refinery blazing – splendid stuff for the newsreel. I took my own route, arrived down at the target, and looked across the Loire to find the refinery absolutely untouched. I went straight across and attacked it – we had a rear facing camera which confirmed I had indeed hit it. No 487 Sqn had never seen the target at all, and when Basil Embry saw the film and realised what had happened, he was very angry indeed. I was promoted to squadron leader and became a flight commander in No 487 Sqn.'

More Mosquito units were allocated to 2nd TAF in late 1943, with No 613 'City of Manchester' Sqn swapping Mustang Is for FB VIs at Lasham in October. No 305 'Polish' Sqn followed suit in December, trading in its Mitchell IIs for FB VIs and joining No 613 Sqn at the Hampshire base. On the last day of 1943, Nos 21, 464 and 487 Sqns took off from Sculthorpe for the last time, bombed Le Ploy, in France, and landed back at their new base at Hunsdon. On 1 February 1944, No 107 Sqn replaced

Sqn Ldr Ian McRitchie DFC, RAAF (left) and Flt Lt R W 'Sammy' Sampson of No 464 Sqn pose by their Mosquito, MM404/SB-T. This aircraft was hit by flak during *Jericho*, forcing a badly wounded McRitchie (he had 26 separate shrapnel wounds) to crash-land his shattered FB VI near Poix. Sampson did not survive the crash (*via John Rayner*)

No 487 Sqn's Plt Offs Maxwell N Sparks (left) and Arthur C Dunlop (navigator) crewed HX982/EG-T during *Jericho*. Their FB VI also flew with Nos 613, 464 and 21 Sqns during its brief operational life. It was finally written off by a crew from the latter unit at Gravesend on 18 April 1944 (*A Dunlop via J Rayner*)

its Bostons with Mosquito FB VIs and moved to Lasham. On 14 February No 226 Sqn also moved south to Hartford Bridge, although this unit retained its Mitchell II/IIIs until war's end.

The Mosquito FB VI boasted the same armament as the fighter version, but had the additional capability of being able to carry two 500-lb bombs in the rear half of the bomb bay – the forward half was taken up with cannon breeches. Wing racks were fitted to carry two 50-gallon drop tanks or a further two 500-lb bombs. In all, crews could carry out a round trip of 1000 miles carrying 4000 rounds of .303 ammunition, 1000 rounds of cannon shell and 2000 lbs of bombs, and still be able to cruise at between 255-325 mph.

During January-February 1944 the Mosquito FB VI units were kept busy destroying V1 flying-bomb launch sites in the Pas de Calais. No 613 Sqn pilot Ron Smith remembers the *Noball* or *Crossbow* operations, as they were code-named;

'The method of attack was to fly out at low level to the target area in loose formation in boxes of four or five aircraft, pull up to 3500 ft, peel off individually, dive down steeply to 1500 ft, release your four 500-lb bombs and return to base at low level. Our aircraft carried no bomb sights, so bombs were dropped at the crew's judgement. Most used the position of the target vis-a-vis the gunsight to decide when to release – taking into account the speed of the aircraft and the angle of the dive. It was simply a matter of practice and experience, and the end results were generally satisfactory. These targets were usually heavily defended by light ack-ack, and losses were experienced as well as numerous aircraft damaged.'

On average, Mosquito units destroyed one *Crossbow* site for each 39.8 tons of bombs dropped, compared with an average of 165.4 tons for the B-17, 182 tons for the Mitchell and 219 tons for the B-26. On occasion, 2nd TAF Mosquitoes were assisted in their attacks against *Noball* sites by two PFF Mosquitoes fitted with *Oboe*, with fighter escort provided by Spitfires. However, this technique meant that they had to fly in tight formation – straight and level – for ten minutes until bomb release, which made them easy targets for flak gunners!

AND THE WALLS CAME TUMBLING DOWN

Two notable pin-point raids were carried out in early 1944, the first of these being Operation *Jericho*, which targeted Amiens Prison. Over 700 French prisoners were known to be incarcerated inside this facility, and British Intelligence had discovered that some of the inmates were to be executed by the Germans on 19 February. 2nd TAF was therefore instructed to attack the prison 24 hours prior to the executions taking place. This task fell to No 140 Wing's Nos 487 and 464 Sqns, who were led on the raid by Grp Capt Percy Pickard and his navigator, Flt Lt 'Pete' Broadley, in the latter squadron's 'F-Freddie' (SB-F). The Mosquitoes took off from Hunsdon in terrible weather, each aircraft carrying 11-second delayed-fuse bombs to breach the prison's 20 ft high and 3 ft thick walls – it was also calculated that the concussion from the detonations would open the cell doors to give most of the prisoners a chance to escape. If Nos 487 and 464 Sqns failed in their mission, then FB VIs of No 21 Sqn, led by Wg Cdr I G 'Daddy' Dale, had orders to destroy the target. By the time the formation crossed the French coast, seven FB VIs and one of the three Typhoon squadrons sent to escort the Mosquitoes had aborted.

At precisely 12.01 pm, with the guards sat down to eat their lunch, bombs from 11 Mosquitoes hit the prison. The first bomb blew in almost all the doors and breached one of the outer walls. Flt Lt Tony Wickham, flying DZ414 (the FPU B Mk IV), made three passes over the burning prison to allow Plt Off Leigh Howard to film the flight of some 255 of the 700 prisoners held captive – 182 of them were later recaptured, whilst some of the 37 prisoners who died during the raid were machine-gunned to death by the sentries. Fifty German guards also died. Almost immediately after leaving the target 'F-Freddie' was shot down by a Fw 190 of II./JG 26, carrying Pickard and Broadley to their deaths, whilst No 464 Sqn's Sqn Ldr Ian McRitchie, RAAF, had his Mosquito peppered with flak. Despite being wounded in 26 places, the Australian pilot managed to crash-land his stricken FB VI near Poix, but his navigator, Flt Lt R W 'Sammy' Sampson, did not survive.

The second precision raid was carried out on 11 April by six FB VIs of No 613 Sqn against the five-storey, 95-ft high, Kunstzaal

No 487 Sqn crews who took part in the Amiens raid are interviewed by the BBC. Top, from left to right, Plt Off D R 'Bob' Fowler (pilot of HX974/EG-J), Plt Off M Barriball, Plt Off M L S Darrall (pilot of HX909/EG-C). Bottom, from left to right, Robin Miller, New Zealand War Correspondent, Plt Off Max Sparks (pilot of HX982/EG-T), David Bernard (BBC) and Plt Off F Stevenson (Darrall's navigator for the operation) (*via John Rayner*)

FB VIs 'T', 'V' and 'D' of No 487 Sqn were photographed on 29 February 1944 each carrying two 500-lb bombs beneath their wings. None of these aircraft had participated in the Amiens prison raid, staged earlier that month (*via GMS*)

This close up shot shows MM417/EG-T as featured in the three-ship formation seen on the previous page. This aircraft was written off on 26 March 1944 after suffering a heavy landing at Hunsdon as a result of flak damage inflicted over the Les Hayes V1 site

Flt Lts Tony Wickham DFC (left) and B T 'Banger' Good, No 21 'City Of Norwich' Sqn's Armaments Officer, pose for the *Illustrated London News* photographer at Thorney Island on 19 December 1944 in front of FB VI 'Kay'. Wickham had participated in the 30 January 1943 daylight raid on Berlin, and went on to serve in No 618 Sqn on the *Highball* project, before being posted to No 21 Sqn, along with his navigator, Plt Off W E D Makin, on 8 September 1944. On 18 February 1944, Wickham flew the FPU's B IV DZ414 on the Amiens raid, making three passes over the burning prison so that his cameraman, Plt Off Leigh Howard, could film the flight of some 255 of the 700 prisoners held captive (*via Les Bulmer*)

Kleizkamp Art Gallery in The Hague, which had been occupied by the Gestapo and used to house the Dutch Central Population Registry, as well as duplicates of all legally issued Dutch personal identity papers. The unit's OC, Wg Cdr R N Bateson DFC, led the operation in FB VI LR355, whilst his 'number two' in the second pair was Flt Lt Ron Smith in HP927;

'I was completely occupied by both flying the aircraft at very low level in formation and listening to my navigator, Flg Off John Hepworth, on what landmark to expect next. The way in was deliberately flown in a roundabout fashion in order to confuse the enemy in respect to our objective, and thus achieve maximum surprise. The first pair, led by the CO, had 30-second delayed action HE bombs, so we in the second pair, led by Sqn Ldr Charles Newman and Flt Lt F G Trevers, had to circle Lake Gouda in order to burn up all the exposed paper work released by the initial explosions. The third pair, led by Flt Lt Vic Hester and Flg Off R Birkett, finished off the mission by dropping HE and incendiary bombs.

'My final recollection is of coming out over playing fields filled with footballers, before crossing the coast north of the city and being escorted home by waiting Spitfires. For his leadership of this operation, Wg Cdr Bateson (who put his bombs literally through the front door!) was awarded the DSO and received the Dutch Flying Cross from Prince Bernhard of The Netherlands.'

The building was destroyed, as were the majority of the identity papers. However, 61 civilians were killed, 24 seriously injured and 43 slightly injured. An Air Ministry bulletin later described the raid as 'probably the most brilliant feat of low-level precision bombing of the war'. During April-May FB VIs of 2nd TAF continued to hit German targets in France and the Low Countries in the build up to D-Day. Ron Smith adds;

'On the night of the D-Day landings, and for many nights afterwards, our chief role was patrolling over, and behind, enemy lines, attacking troop movements and anything in the way of enemy activity on the ground. Our mode of entry and exit was via the sea corridor between Alderney and the Cherbourg Peninsular, entering France at Granville and then making our way to the "Tennis Court", which was our patrol area. During the period 5 June to 11 July, John and I completed 17 operational sorties, all at night. In June these sorties were all in the Normandy area, attacking roads, bridges, marshalling yards and any lights or movements seen. Sometimes we would rendezvous with Mitchells, who would drop

flares for us in order to improve target visibility.'

Each navigational log had its own story to tell. E S Gates of No 613 Sqn recalls;

'That pitch black night when, unfavourably placed, we dived steeply to attack a light and saw the dark silhouettes of trees rush past us on our starboard side as we abruptly climbed, a split-second away from oblivion. Then there was that occasion when, working as an intruder pair, Frankie Reede dropped a flare as we took up a favourable position to attack the target. Naked under the yellow light, and near blinded by its brilliance, we were engulfed

by a tangled trellis of coloured tracer shells. Identifying nothing, and with the instincts of self-preservation uppermost in our minds, we dived away into the blackness beyond the flare.'

Until suitable airstrips could be made ready, the Mosquito wings flew operations from Thorney Island and Lasham. During this time some spectacular pinpoint daylight raids against specific buildings were flown. For example, on Bastille Day (14 July 1944) a large German Army barracks at Bonneuil Matours, near Poitiers, was attacked by 18 FB VIs of Nos 21, 487 and 464 Sqns. The Mosquitoes dropped nine tons of bombs (fused for 25 seconds' delay) in a series of shallow dives, destroying six buildings inside a rectangle of just 170 ft by 100ft – at least 150 soldiers were killed. On 1 August a follow up raid involving 24 Mosquito FB.VIs of Nos 487 and 21 Sqns, escorted by Mustangs, was made on the Caserne des Dunes barracks at Potiers, where about 2000 Germans were billeted. On 2 August, 23 FB VIs of Nos 107 and 305 Sqns attacked both the SS police HQ at Chateau de Fou, south of Chatellerault, and Chateau Maulny, which housed a school for saboteurs. No 613 Sqn, meanwhile, bombed a chateau in Normandy which was serving as a rest home for German submariners.

On 19 August 14 FB VI crews from No 613 Sqn were led by Sqn Ldr Charles Newman on a daring low level attack on a school building at Egletons, 50 miles south-east of Limoges, which British Intelligence believed was in use as an SS barracks. As usual, AVM Basil Embry and Grp Capt Bower went along to observe the squadron in action. Fourteen of the Mosquitoes located and bombed the target, scoring at least 20 direct hits which all but destroyed the school. One FB VI was struck in the starboard engine by flak over the target area and had to crash-land in France, but the crew returned to the squadron just five days later.

On 25/26 August No 138 Wing took part in all-out attacks in the Rouen area against troop concentrations and convoys of vehicles that were attempting to retreat across the Seine. Sorties continued on the night of 30 August against railways in the Saarbourg and Strassburg areas, followed 24 hours later by a raid on a huge petrol dump at Nomency, near

No 613 'City of Manchester' Sqn flew its first Mosquito operation from Hartford Bridge on 31 December 1943, attacking a V1 site in northern France. On 11 April 1944 the unit sent six FB VIs (led by Wg Cdr R N 'Pin Point' Bateson) to destroy the Kunstzaal Kleizkamp, a five-storey, 90-ft high, central registry building in The Hague which contained Gestapo records of the Dutch Resistance. This shot shows the immediate aftermath of the attack as seen out the rear of a fleeing FB VI (*via Carl Bartram*)

Armourers fit a 250-lb bomb to the wing of FB VI LR355/'H' of No 613 Sqn. This aircraft was still serving with the unit when it was written off in a crash-landing following an engine failure on 1 August 1944

FB VI LR366 of No 613 Sqn is
rearmed and refuelled on a damp
dispersal at Lasham on 7 February
1944. This aircraft went on to serve
with No 107 Sqn later in the year,
but was lost over Arnhem on 17
September 1944 – the opening day
of Operation *Market Garden*. LR366
was hit by flak, caught fire and
crashed near to the enemy position
it had been attacking
(*via Phil Jarrett*)

A line up of No 464 Sqn FB VIs at
Thorney Island in mid-1944. During
April-May of that year Mosquitoes
of 2nd TAF continued their bombing
of targets in France and the Low
Countries as part of the build up to
D-Day. In June, sorties were flown
exclusively over the Normandy area
against roads, bridges, marshalling
yards and any vehicles seen on the
move (*A Thomas via S Howe*)

Nancy. Twelve FB VIs of No 464 Sqn also attacked a dozen petrol trains
near Chagney, their strafing and bombing runs at heights of between 20
to 200 ft causing widespread destruction.

On 17 September, as part of Operation *Market Garden* (the airborne
invasion of Holland), 32 FB VIs from Nos 107 and 613 Sqns within No
138 Wing attacked the barracks at Arnhem, while No 21 Sqn bombed
three school buildings in the centre of Nijmegen which were being used
by the German garrison.

LOW-LEVEL TO AARHUS

As the Allied armies pushed further into western Europe, more precision
attacks were ordered. On 31 October Nos 21, 464 and 487 Sqns
despatched a total of 25 FB VIs (each carrying 11-second delayed action
bombs and escorted by eight Mustang IIIs of No 315 'Polish' Sqn) on a
daring low level attack on Aarhus University, which housed the Gestapo
HQ for the whole of Jutland, in Denmark. College No 4 was also the HQ
of the SD, the Nazi Party's police service. Australian Ern Dunkley, who
flew one of the No 464 Sqn FB VIs sent on the raid, recalls;

'The University of Aarhus consisted of four or five buildings just next

FB VI LR356/YH-Y (flown by Sqn Ldr Tony Carlisle) of No 21 Sqn is seen in planform from a second Mosquito at 20,000 ft over a *Noball* target in 1944. Whilst operating as part of No 140 Wing, 2nd TAF, this unit gained a reputation for pin-point bombing raids during 1944/45. On 6 February 1945 the squadron moved to Rosiéres-en-Santerre, in France, this airfield being the first in a series of continental bases used by the unit until war's end. LR356 completed two tours with No 21 Sqn, in between which was sandwiched a spell with No 613 Sqn. Returned to the latter unit after completing its second tour with No 21 Sqn, LR356 was lost on a night intruder mission over north-west Germany on 2 February 1945 (*via Les Bulmer*)

to an autobahn, which ran ten miles in a straight line up to it. We all crossed the Channel together and made landfall at a lake, where we made a rate one turn. The first six aircraft took off for the target, followed at short intervals by the remaining three boxes of six. It was a very well planned run really, except that the wind was blowing right down the autobahn. The blokes who went in first had a good picture of the target, whereas those following had to deal with dust and smoke. By the time we got there the place was a mess. There was a hospital not far along the road on the other side, and although a lot of people must have got a shock from the noise, not a single bomb landed in the hospital area. On the way home I lost track of our CO (Wg Cdr A W Langton DFC) and had called over the radio, "Has anyone seen the old man?" He came back saying, "We are not home yet. Shut up!" The flight took 4 hours and 45 minutes.'

The operation, which was led by Hurricane ace Grp Capt Peter Wykeham-Barnes, was carried out at such a low altitude that Sqn Ldr F H Denton of No 487 Sqn hit the roof of the building, losing his tail wheel and the port half of the tailplane. Despite the damage, he nursed the FB VI safely back across the North Sea to England. Inside one of the buildings, 40-year-old Pastor Sandbäk, who had been arrested in September on suspicion of complicity in acts of sabotage, was about to endure his final interrogation – he had survived 39 hours without any rest, following days of whipping and the tightening of string around his handcuffs;

'Suddenly, we heard the whine of the first exploding bomb while the planes thundered across the University. The face of my interrogator – a German named Werner – was as pale as death from fright. He and his assistants ran without thinking of me. I saw them run down a passage to the right, and instinctively I went down to the left. This saved my life. Shortly afterwards the whole building collapsed. Werner and his two assistants were killed. I heard two bangs and everything went blank. When I awoke again I was buried under bricks.'

In July-August 1944, FB VIs of 2nd TAF were called upon to make three pinpoint raids against barracks occupied by the 158th Security Regiment near the town of Poitiers, in France, after they had massacred captured Maquis and SAS troops at a site nearby. On Bastille Day, 14 July 1944, Hurricane ace Grp Capt Peter Wykeham-Barnes DSO*, DFC (pictured) led Nos 487 and 464 Sqns in an attack by 18 FB VIs on six buildings inside a rectangle just 170 ft x 100 ft at Bonneuil Matours, near Poitiers. The Mosquitoes destroyed the barracks with nine tons of bombs, dropped in shallow dives (*Derek Carter Collection*)

On 30 July 1944 the Caserne des Dunes barracks at Poitiers was destroyed by Mosquitoes, and on 2 August the survivors of the notorious 158th Security Regiment – now billeted in the Chateau de Fou (pictured), an SS police HQ south of Chatellerault – were killed when the barracks was bombed by 23 FB VIs drawn from Nos 107 and 305 Sqns. It is estimated that 80 per cent of the regiment were killed as a result of the three separate raids (*Vic Hester*)

Pastor Sandbäk was later spirited across the border to neutral Sweden. Among the 110 to 175 Germans estimated to have been killed in the raid was 'Kriminal rat' Schwitzgiebel, head of the Gestapo in Jutland.

By November 1944 No 138 Wing's Nos 107, 305 and 613 Sqns had finally arrived in France to be based at Epinoy, near Cambrai. Meanwhile, Nos 21, 464 and 487 Sqns initially remained behind at Thorney Island, but in December the Australian and New Zealand units both sent advance detachments to Rosiäres-en-Santerre, in France, and by February 1945 all three squadrons were permanently based there.

By this stage of the war the enemy was being bombed both day and night. Nocturnal FB VIs also reaped a rich harvest of enemy aircraft, and continued to harrass troop movements behind the German thrust in the Ardennes, as well as flying close support sorties over the frontline. The Luftwaffe was powerless to stop their inexorable advance westwards, and

On 19 August 1944, 15 FB VIs of No 613 Sqn (led by Sqn Ldr Charles Newman) attacked a Gestapo HQ housed in a former school building at Egeltons, some 50 miles south-east of Limoges – intelligence on the site also indicated that the school was being used as a barracks for SS troops. The Mosquitoes located the target and bombed from low level, scoring at least 20 direct hits which left the building almost completely destroyed (*Vic Hester*)

even Operation *Bodenplatte* (which saw some 850+ fighters attack 27 airfields in northern France, Belgium and southern Holland early on New Year's Day) failed to halt the Allies.

Throughout January-March 1945, Nos 138 and 140 Wings, along with all the other Allied tactical units, continued the offensive on most nights by attacking German road and rail transport when possible, and bombing rail junctions using *Gee* when bad weather prevented visual sightings. The Mosquito coped well with the upturn in operations, as Flt Lt Eric Atkins (a pilot with No 305 'Polish' Sqn) remembers;

'Being small and light, the Mosquito could fall foul to bad weather. On the other hand, in emergency conditions, when caught in flak or searchlights, or when being attacked by enemy aircraft, it could be flung around the sky in almost impossible manoeuvres. The Mosquito responded to the controls like a thoroughbred racehorse, with speed, precision and a sixth sense of judgement linked to that of the pilot. I have also known the FB VI to turn in such a tight circle at night, in order to get away from searchlights and flak, that it virtually "disappeared up its own orifice".

'A Mosquito could fly well on one engine, providing you had the speed and height to gain level flight over a long distance. Many a Mosquito pilot flew back from Germany on one engine, but the landing could be tricky, and you never knew whether the other engine would overheat and pack up! A Mosquito would also do a safe belly landing, providing you remembered to come in without any undercarriage and flaps – the latter would invariably cause it to turn over. I landed at night on a grass 'drome at Epinoy, France, with no undercarriage, no flaps and a bomb aboard! The only annoying thing was that the ambulance and MO took over half an hour to reach us – they were waiting to see whether the bomb went off! The aircraft had only minor damage and was soon returned to service again. Other Mosquitoes landed with half a wing missing.

No 613 Sqn's AC1 Phillip Beck and LAC E Kerslake – the 'boys with the gen' – refill FB VI 'W's' oxygen tanks in preparation for a raid on Berlin (Flight *via Phillip Beck*)

B Mk IV DZ383/? was used by the FPU within No 138 Wing, 2nd TAF. The nose of the bomber was modified so as to be mostly made of perspex or glass panels, which allowed the cameraman to squat and shoot his cine films from virtually any angle. A 400f reel camera, fixed to shoot straight ahead, was also fitted into the aircraft. It was aimed by the pilot through the use of a simple gunsight installed in the cockpit. On 17 September 1944, DZ383 was flown by Flt Lt Vic A Hester (and cameraman Ted Moore) of No 613 Sqn during an attack on a barracks at Arnhem ahead of the *Market Garden* operation. After dropping its bomb, the B Mk IV was used as a photographic mount to capture the airborne assault on film (*via Vic Hester*)

FB VIs 'B' and 'H' of No 613 Sqn are seen at A75/Cambrai-Epinoy, in France, in late 1944. The squadron had moved here, together with Nos 107 and 305 Sqns within No 138 Wing, in November 1944 in order to be closer to the frontline for their harrassing missions against German units retreating further eastwards (*Philip Beck*)

On 31 October 1944 25 FB VIs from Nos 21, 464 and 487 Sqs destroyed the Gestapo HQ at Aarhus University (and the incriminating records held within its buildings), in Denmark. The Mosquitoes used 11-second delayed-action fuse 500-lb bombs on this mission, which was led led by Grp Capt Peter Wykeham-Barnes. For low level operations, 500-lb bombs were usually fused to detonate between eight and fourteen seconds after being dropped, thus allowing the Mosquito to get far enough away from the blast. It also meant that a bomb could successfully penetrate a building before exploding. When 2nd TAF started performing these pinpoint raids, it was quickly found that the Mosquitoes were flying so low that their bombs were hitting the target before the safe/live mechanism had 'unwound', thus arming the bomb for detonation. Armourers cured the problem by simply cutting the thread of the fuse from four inches to about two so that the bomb became live virtually from the moment it left the aircraft! (*Derek Carter*)

'Despite its wooden construction the Mosquito had strength and endurance, and was easier to repair – you simply spliced another wing on! The speed of the Mosquito also meant that the operational time was less (unless you were "Ranging"), and the turn-around time was such that when German light vehicles were piled up around Rouen, an all-night attack was called. We did three operations in one night, landing, refuelling, rearming and away again – a dusk to dawn hat-trick!'

On 22 February 1945 Mosquito squadrons participated in Operation *Clarion* – a maximum daylight effort to deliver the *coup de grace* to the German transport system. Altogether, some 9000 Allied aircraft were involved in attacks on enemy railway stations, trains and engines, cross roads, bridges, ships and barges on canals and rivers, stores and other targets. P D Morris, a pilot with No 613 Sqn, recalls;

'The area given to Ron Parfitt (my navigator) and I to patrol was the very north of Germany up in Schleswig Holstein, near the Danish border. Our job was to patrol a large area and bomb, machine gun and cannon any enemy transport or personnel we spotted. After being able to cause a little havoc on various targets, the time came for us to make our way home. As we flew at low-level over fields separated by dykes that were at much the same height as us, a German soldier appeared at the top of a dyke some 300 yards ahead of us and proceeded to fire his gun in our direction. I was armed with both four machine guns and four cannon, and I took careful aim and pulled both triggers. My guns remained completely silent! However, I was determined to frighten him badly, so I passed over him at a few feet and saw him fall flat on his face. Once past the soldier I tried the guns again, and they fired perfectly!'

Clarion was to be the last time that the Mosquitoes operated in daylight in such numbers – Nos 138 and 140 Wings lost nine FB VIs, and many more were damaged.

OPERATION *CARTHAGE*

In March 1945 No 140 Wing was tasked with another daring operation, this time on the Shellhaus Gestapo HQ in Copenhagen. Having grown wise to the vulnerability of their buildings to precision bombing attacks, the Germans installed cells in the top storey of the

Shellhaus and moved in 26 resistance and political prisoners. However, British Intelligence learned that the resistance fighters preferred to be killed by RAF bombs than be shot by the Gestapo, so Operation *Carthage* went ahead from Fersfield, Norfolk, on 21 March 1945. Flying FB VI RS570, Grp Capt R N 'Bob' Bateson DSO, DFC, AFC and the leading tactical navigator, Sqn Ldr Ted Sismore DSO, DFC, led 18 Mosquitoes in three waves – each wave comprised six-seven aircraft in echelon-starboard formation. The leading two FB VIs in the first wave carried 30-second delayed-action bombs, whilst the rest were loaded with 11-second delayed-action devices. Two Film Photographic Unit Mosquitoes (each carrying two 500-lb HE bombs and two 500-lb M.76 incendiaries) accompanied the FB VIs at minimum height to Copenhagen – the formation was escorted by 28 Mustang IIIs.

Four Mosquitoes were lost during the raid including SZ977, which was being flown by No 21 Sqn's OC, Wg Cdr Peter Kleboe, DSO, DFC, AFC – he was flying as the fourth FB VI in the first wave, behind Bateson/Sismore, Carlisle/Ingram (PZ306) and Embry/Clapham (PZ222). Just 800 yards from the target, Kleboe hit a 130-ft high floodlight pylon in a marshalling yard and went into a vertical dive. Flt Lt T M 'Mac' Hetherington, RCAF, and Flt Lt J K Bell were in the No 6 position in

An armourer hoists a 500-lb bomb into position aboard an FB VI during the winter of 1944-45. This Mosquito variant could carry two 500-lb bombs in the rear half of the bomb bay only, as the forward half was taken up with cannon breeches (*via GMS*)

FB VIs 'D', 'X' and PZ306/Y (the latter being flown here by Sqn Ldr A F Carlisle) of No 21 Sqn, as photographed from B Mk IV DZ383/? during high-level formation practice and checks on wing tanks on 15 March 1945. This sortie was flown in preparation for the Shellhaus raid on 21 March 1945 – 'D' and 'X' were not used on the latter operation. PZ306 flew exclusively with this unit in 1944/45, before being sold to an undisclosed buyer in November 1946 (*Mrs A Carlisle via Derek Carter*)

On 21 March 1945, FB VIs of No 140 Wing attacked and destroyed the Shellhaus Gestapo building in Copenhagen, which contained 26 Danish resistance prisoners on the top floor, releasing 18 of them. To the lower right of the building (seen smoking centre right), skirting the rooftops, is B Mk IV DZ414/'O-Orange', crewed by Flt Lt K L Greenwood and Flg Off E Moore of No 487 Sqn. A veteran of virtually all the great low level Mosquito raids of 1944/45, plus tours with the original 'shallow divers' of Nos 105, 109 and 139 Sqns in 1942/43, DZ414 survived the war and was eventually struck off charge on 16 October 1946 (*via Derek Carter*)

Sqn Ldr Ted Sismore DSO, DFC*, AFC was 'Bob' Bateson's navigator in FB VI RS570/EG-X during the Shellhaus raid. Although this crew pairing belonged to No 21 Sqn, their mount was actually loaned from No 487 Sqn (*Derek Carter Collection*)

HR162, behind and to the right side of Kleboe. The Canadian observed;

'We watched each other and attempted to follow the leader by "biting hard into his tail", whilst at the same time staying clear of his slipstream. We followed each other like shadows. We were altogether, some twelve feet lower than the first three aircraft. We knew that we had to turn, but apparently Wg Cdr Kleboe had not seen the pylon, or had reacted too slowly. Suddenly, through the side window I observed Kleboe's aircraft climb at a very steep angle and fall off to port. Sqn Ldr A C Henderson (in LR388, the fifth Mosquito in the formation) and I instinctively threw our aircraft to starboard and continued on towards the target.'

Flt Lt Ken Greenwood, who was flying DZ414 'Q-Query' (the FPU Mosquito) on the port side of Kleboe's aircraft, adds;

'Some 10-15 seconds before the accident, bomb doors had been opened, copying the leader. Kleboe's aircraft lost height (some 15 ft), and I suppose by peripheral vision I saw the pylon and realised that he was going to fly into it. As the aircraft struck the pylon, part of the port engine was damaged. The Mosquito rose almost vertically and then climbed rapidly to port. I had to take violent evasive action to prevent a mid-air collision, and swung hard to port.'

Kleboe's two bombs struck a building in Sdr Boulevard (one failed to explode) and 11 civilians were killed, whilst his aircraft crashed near the Jeanne d'Arc school in a pall of black smoke. Both the pilot and his navigator, Flg Off Reg Hall, RCAF, died instantly.

After getting their bombs away, the first wave scattered and exited Copenhagen at roof top height. Bateson and Sismore put their bombs through the first and second floors of the Shellhaus, whilst AVM Embry/Sqn Ldr Peter Clapham and Sqn Ldr Tony Carlisle/Flt Lt Rex Ingram also bombed successfully. Henderson and 'Mac' Hetherington pierced the roof of the target, although the former had to take evasion action and climb over Embry's aircraft, which had strayed across his flightpath, before dropping his bombs – Henderson's navigator, Bill Moore, commented, 'Look. The old man's going sightseeing!'

The second wave of six Mosquitoes hailed from No 464 Sqn RAAF, their OC, Wg Cdr Bob Iredale DSO, DFC, RAAF, leading the way in SZ968, along with his navigator Flg Off B J Standish. Arriving over Copenhagen some two minutes behind the first wave, the Australians found their path criss-crossed by flak. The leading three crews were also distracted by the smoke pall rising from Kleboe's wrecked aircraft, as this was far thicker than that emanating from the Shellhaus. Confusion reigned, and the force was split into two. A split-second decision had to be made, so Iredale broke off his attack, circled to come in again, and got his bombs away on the east end of the Shellhaus. In the confusion, it appears that one Mosquito bombed the Jeanne d'Arc school by mistake.

Flt Lt Knowle Shrimpton and Flg Off Peter Lake, RAAF, also orbited the target twice in PZ353, as the former explains;

'We came up to the lake where we would drop our wing tanks. I had to

Flg Off Peter Lake DFC, RAAF (left) and Flt Lt W Knowle Shrimpton DFC participated in both the Aarhus and the Shellhaus raids with No 464 Sqn (*Derek Carter Collection*)

This amazing photograph shows Shrimpton and Lake fly low over Søborg, just north of Copenhagen, in FB VI PZ353/SB-G during the raid on the Shellhaus on 21 March 1945. They made two orbits of the target area and, seeing that the building was already well damaged and on fire, flew back with their bomb load intact, rather than risk killing further prisoners. As with FB VI MM412, featured on page 52 of this chapter, PZ353 survived both its tour with No 464 Sqn and time with No 1 Overseas Ferry Unit, before eventually being sold to the Yugoslav Air Force in October 1952 (*Toxvaerd Foto via Derek Carter*)

American Flg Off R E 'Bob' Kirpatrick of No 21 Sqn was the pilot of the FPU B Mk IV Series II DZ383/'Q-Query' during the Shellhaus raid (*Derek Carter Collection*)

Flg Off Kirkpatrick (left) and his navigator-cameraman, Sgt R Hearne of No 4 FPU, pose in front of the flak-damaged DZ383 at Rackheath, in Norfolk, where they had force-landed without flaps or brakes after their long flight back from Denmark. This aircraft was one of two FPU Mosquitoes sent on the Shellhaus raid (*Mrs S Hearne via Derek Carter*)

keep the Mosquito straight and level during this part of the operation – no skidding – so that the tanks would fall cleanly without rolling into the tailplane. This was not easy due to the extremely high turbulence. Peter concentrated on map reading and I focussed on accurate flying. I prayed that he had memorised the track. Then, on the outskirts of the city, I recognised the first landmark shown on the briefing model. Flying became precise – height 50 ft, engine revs and boost. We wanted 320 mph, but settled for 305-310, which was all we could get. I set the bomb fuses and opened the bomb bay doors. We were getting close. Flak looped over the target from the right, with not much room over Shellhaus.

'The next event was a shock. Peter yelled, "Don't bomb, smoke to port!" He signalled to me that something was wrong. Were we on target? This all took place some 10-15 seconds from what we believed to be the target. Enough time to see that the building in question was not damaged, but insufficient time to evaluate all the facts. I aborted the attack, cleared the building, and closed the bomb doors. Throttling back and keeping low, I commenced a left-hand orbit. After a moment we had left the flak area and I reduced the rate of turn. We then assessed the situation and made a plan. The building which we were confident was the target was not damaged, being devoid of fire or smoke. We decided that the preceding aircraft had probably bombed the wrong target. Was the fire a decoy?

'We decided to get ourselves into position for another run up to the target. Then, realising that we were alone without orientation of our position, we commenced another orbit. After about 325° we became re-orientated, firstly by Peter's recognition of the run-up track, and as a result of that, my identification of the target. Here, we determined that Shellhaus had been hit as we could see dust and smoke. I continued to turn onto the run-up, and as we came in we agreed that the job had been done. We observed heavy damage to the base of the building and dust and smoke. More bombs might have unnecessarily endangered the Danes in the Shellhaus, so we aborted. Later, on the flight home, we felt a sense of failure, or at least disappointment, that we still had our bombs aboard.'

Meanwhile, the three FB VIs in 'Blue Section' (led by Flt Lt Archie Smith/Flt Sgt E L Green in PZ309), together with the Mustang escort, had circled the area to clarify their position. During their first orbit some Mosquitoes were too far left of the target, leaving only those aircraft closest to Shellhaus able to drop their bombs. Smith circled the target twice more before bombing, his ordnance striking the outside of the east wing and destroying a pillbox on the corner of the building. The two other FB VIs – SZ999 (Flg Offs 'Shorty' Dawson, RAAF/F T Murray) and RS609 (Flg Off 'Spike' Palmer, RAAF/Sub-Lt H H Becker, a Norwegian) – were hit by flak and forced to ditch in the sea. There were no survivors.

The third wave, consisting of the six No 487 Sqn, RNZAF, FB VIs (led by Wg Cdr F H Denton, with Flg Off A J Coe, in PZ402) had navigation problems and approached the target area from the north-east – completely the wrong direction. All except Denton, who located Shellhaus but saw so much damage already that he aborted his attack and jettisoned his bombs in the sea, bombed the area around the Jeanne d'Arc school by mistake. The building was destroyed and 86 of the 482 children inside were killed, with a further 67 wounded – 16 adults also died and 35 were wounded, plus several people were killed around the target area itself.

Denton nursed his flak-damaged FB VI back to England, where he executed a perfect belly landing, whilst Flt Lt Dempsey and Flt Sgt Paige flew PZ462 home (a distance of 400 miles) on one engine, the second Merlin having been damaged by a single bullet in its coolant system. DZ383 'Q-Query' (the second FPU aircraft, flown by American Flg Off R E 'Bob' Kirkpatrick with Sgt R Hearne) of No 21 Sqn also limped home after taking a flak hit over the target with the third wave. Kirkpatrick recalls;

'As we approached the city I could see a huge pall of black smoke dead ahead, and, at the same time, some Mossies in a tight left turn. Our courses were converging. As they straightened out towards the smoke I had only a second to decide to join them close enough to avoid the 11-second delay bombs, or risk a right turn with the cruddy windshield (which had become coated with salt spray low over the North Sea). The Mossies levelled off on track and I tucked in close just as their bomb doors opened. I opened mine and saw their bombs drop just before we entered the smoke. I dropped my bomb load, then got a pretty good wallop in the smoke, and after breaking out, I lost contact with the other Mosquitoes.

'On the outskirts of the city I saw two Mossies at about 3 o'clock on a northerly heading. I joined up with them only to see that one was smoking badly from the starboard engine (NT123 – Flt Lt D V Pattison and Flt Sgt F Pygram's Mosquito had been hit by flak from the cruiser *Nürnburg*, moored in the harbour). The escorting Mosquito waved me off, as without guns I would be just a burden, and their course was not towards England. I turned west just in time to see a sandbagged gun pit with two guns firing at the three of us – we had inadvertantly got close to a large barracks. The best, and quickest, evasion was to go straight towards the gun pit and dive. I opened the bomb doors to get their attention and spoil their aim. As the doors opened the gunners abandoned their weapons and ducked down. We were gone in a flash, flying right over them.'

Pattison and Pygram ditched in the sea close to the Swedish island of Hveen, and although they were seen standing on a wing, they later drowned – no bodies were recovered. Kirkpatrick concludes;

'On the return trip we sweated fuel for over an hour. When we spotted the English coast and then an air base, I went straight in. I got the wheels down, but nothing for flaps or brakes, so I coasted to a stop on the grass by the runway. We had found a B-24 base (Rackheath) near Norwich. We were escorted by MPs to the control tower to explain our presence.'

Four Mosquitoes and two Mustangs failed to return, with nine aircrew being killed. The Shellhaus and Gestapo records were destroyed, and of the 26 prisoners in the building, 18 escaped. Some of those that had survived the attack were injured or killed when they jumped from the fifth floor into the street below. If all the FB VIs' bombs had been dropped, it is doubtful if anyone would have survived. Some 26 Nazis, 30 Danish collaborators and 16 civilians were killed. After the war a memorial was raised to the children and adults killed, and to the Resistance.

No 140 Wing had one more low level pinpoint raid to fly. On 17 April six FB VIs, led by Bateson and Sismore, taxied out for a daylight strike on a school building on the outskirts of Odense which was being used by the Gestapo as an HQ. Basil Embry went along, as usual. The Mosquitoes destroyed the building, and 18 days later Denmark was free. At 0800 hours on 8 May the cease-fire came into effect, and VE-Day was declared.

ABOVE THE WAVES

During World War 2 German capital ships, moored deep within the Norwegian fjords, potentially posed a serious threat to Allied shipping in both home waters and out into the North Atlantic. The vessel which the Royal Navy feared the most was the battleship *Tirpitz*, which had defied conventional bombing raids staged in an effort to sink it. Therefore, on 1 April 1943, just one month before No 617 Sqn's successful attack on the Ruhr dams with *Upkeep* 'bouncing' bombs, No 618 Sqn was formed within Coastal Command at Skitten, near Wick. Established under strict secrecy, the squadron's sole purpose was to use Dr Barnes Wallis' *Highball* weapon in a series of strikes code-named Operation *Servant* aimed at sinking both the *Tirpitz* and other capital ships at sea. *Highball* weighed 950 lbs (600 lbs of which was the explosive charge itself), and boasted a diameter of 35 inches – some 9 inches smaller than the 11,000-lb *Upkeep* bomb, which had a charge weight of 7000 lbs. No 618 Sqn was issued with modified B Mk IVs, each aircraft carrying two *Highballs* which they launched at low level with a back spin of approximately 500 rpm at a distance of three-quarters of a mile from the target.

Using a nucleus of 19 crews (including 11 crews from Nos 105 and 139 Sqns, as well as their aircraft), No 618 Sqn spent much of 1943 learning how to drop the *Highballs*. Despite myriad training flights, by the eve of the planned 15 May attack on the *Tirpitz* only six suitably-modified B Mk IVs had arrived at Skitten, so the strike was abandoned.

Highball trials continued unabated, however, with No 618 Sqn now earmarked for the Pacific theatre, where its mission would be to use its unique weapons against the Japanese fleet at Truk – because of the distance involved, the Mosquito crews were told they would have to operate from an aircraft carrier! Ten *Highball* crews and ten PR crews, whose task it would be to find the Japanese ships, were trained on carriers using Bar-

HJ732/G (G denoted that the aircraft was secret and had to be guarded at all times), which served as the prototype FB XVIII 'Tsetse', had initially been built as an FB VI Series I aircraft. Note the muzzle of the 'six pounder' 57 mm Molins gun protruding from beneath the quartet of Browning .303-in machine guns, which were later halved in number in an effort to save weight, and thus allow more fuel to be carried. 'Tsetses' operated exclusively with No 618 Sqn (Special Detachment) on anti-submarine, ground attack and anti-shipping strikes during 1943-44 (*BAe via GMS*)

racuda IIs, and on 31 October 24 B Mk IVs and three PR XVIs were ferried out to the Pacific on two escort carriers, arriving in Melbourne, on 23 December 1944. However, the Japanese ships had by now been sunk, so the unit saw out the rest of the war in Australia without ever seeing action. No 618 Sqn finally left for the return trip to England on VE-Day, leaving its aircraft behind.

Prior to its posting to Australia, No 618 Sqn had detached five crews to the Beaufighter Mk X-equipped No 248 Sqn at Predannack to operate Mk XVIII 'Tsetse' Mosquitoes – so named because of the 57 mm Molins automatic weapon installed in the nose of the aircraft in place of the standard quartet of 20 mm cannon. Fitted primarily for use against surfaced U-boats, the gun was fed armour-plated HE 6-lb shells, capped with tracer, from an arc-shaped magazine that could hold 24 rounds. Positioned vertically about midships, the magazine slotted the shells directly into the gun's

Proudly wearing the Norwegian flag, this weathered FB VI was part of No 333 Sqn's 'B Flight', based at Banff, in late 1943. It has had nose doors hinged back so as to allow the armourers to reload its .303-in machine guns and 20 mmm cannon. Note the belt of shells for the latter weapons laying on the ground beneath the aircraft (*via Cato Gunnfeldt, Barum – Norway*)

breech block. The latter was located behind the crew, and the barrel extended below the floor of the cockpit, with the muzzle protruding from beneath the nose fairing. Two (or four) .303-in machine guns were retained for both strafing and air combat, and all these guns were aimed through one reflector sight – the firing buttons were positioned on the control column. The Molins gun had a muzzle velocity of 2950 ft per second, and the ideal range from which to open fire was 1800-1500 yards.

'Tsetse' operations began on 24 October 1943 with a patrol by two Mk XVIIIs flown by Sqn Ldr C Rose DFC, DFM and Sgt Cowley, and Flg Off A Bonnett, RCAF, and Plt Off Mc D 'Pickles' McNicol. The former crew was lost on 4 November when they crashed into the sea during an attack on a trawler in the Bay of Biscay. Rose fired two shells, but was either hit by return fire or by a ricochet from one of his own rounds.

The mine-swept channels off the French Atlantic coast which led to U-boat bases at Brest, Lorient, St Nazaire, La Rochelle and Bordeaux were the ideal 'killing grounds' because the water depth was too shallow to permit the U-boats to crash-dive if attacked. On 7 November, Al Bonnett scored hits on U-123, which was returning on the surface to Brest. After the first dive, Bonnett's cannon jammed, so he strafed the U-boat with machine gun fire. Attacking in a Mk XVIII required a dive from about 5000 ft at a 30° angle, with the turn-and-bank indicator dead central – the slightest drift would cause the gun to jam. As a result of this attack, escort vessels were now provided for the U-boats.

By 1 January 1944, No 248 Sqn's Mosquito Conversion Flight had 16 'Tsetses' and four FB VIs on strength, and on 16 February the unit moved to Portreath. It flew its first first interceptor and anti-shipping patrols into the Bay of Biscay just four days later.

On 10 March four FB VIs which had escorted two Mk XVIIIs to an area about 30 miles north of Gijon, on the Spanish coast, tangled with about ten Ju 88s that had been sent to cover a convoy comprising four destroyers and a U-boat. Two Ju 88s were downed by the FB VIs while the 'Tsetses' attacked the convoy. Sqn Ldr Phillips carried out four attacks on the U-boat and Flg Off Turner two. They damaged a destroyer and Phillips downed a Ju 88 with four shells from his Molins gun.

On 25 March, whilst patrolling in the Il de Yen area of the Bay of Biscay, two 'Tsetses' (MM425/L, flown by Flg Offs Doug Turner and Des Curtis, and HX903/I, crewed by Flg Off A H Hilliard and Wt Off J Hoyle) sank U-976, which was returning to St Nazaire with a destroyer and two minesweepers after being recalled from her second war cruise. Flak from the escorts, which were attacked by the four FB VIs of No 248 Sqn (led by Flt Lt L S Dobson) was intense. Turner made four attacks on U-976 and Hilliard one before the vessel submerged, leaving a patch of oil 100 yards long by 30 yards wide on the surface. The survivors were picked up by escorting minesweepers.

LA-V and a second FB VI of No 235 Sqn were photographed from a third Mosquito en route to Norway at their usual height of 50 ft above the waves (day and night). Flt Lt George Lord was the pilot of 'V', whose tail wheel remained extended throughout the sortie (*G A B Lord*)

No 248 Sqn's FB VI LR347 'T-Tommy' was the aircraft used by Flt Lt Stanley G Nunn and Flg Off J M Carlin to attack U-821, a Type VIIC submarine, off Ushant on 10 June 1944. The U-boat, commanded by Oberleutnant Ulrich Knacfuss, was eventually sunk by Liberator EV943/K of No 206 Sqn. On 16 July 1944, 'T-Tommy' made a belly landing at Portreath after sustaining flak damage which had knocked out its port engine. The aircraft was duly repaired and went on to serve with No 8 OTU (*R W Simmons via Andy Thomas*)

On 14 September 1944, Nos 235 and 248 Sqns moved to Scotland to join the Banff Strike Wing for operations against enemy shipping off Norway. On the 28th their aircraft were modified to carry Mk IIIA tapered type rails (made of lengths of tubular steel welded together) and eight RPs with 60-lb Semi-Armour-Piercing heads of the type used in the desert for tank-busting. These did not, however, penetrate the sides of ships, and they were soon replaced with 25-lb solid armour-piercing warheads. Mosquitoes used RPs for the first time on 26 October 1944

Two days later, in the same area, these two 'Tsetse' crews, escorted by six FB VIs of No 248 Sqn (led by Flt Lt J H B Rollett), made attacks on U-769 and U-960, which were en route to La Pallice. A heavy flak barrage was put up by the U-boats' escort of four 'M' Class minesweepers and two *Sperrbrechers* (merchantmen converted to flak ships). Hilliard's Mosquito was hit in the nose by a 37 mm shell, but fortunately the armour plating beneath the instrument panel cushioned the impact and the crew reached Portreath safely – Flt Sgt L A Compton (in LR363/X) crash-landed on his return. U-960, which was badly damaged in the attack, limped into La Pallice for repairs. A year later she was sunk in the Mediterranean through a combination of US destroyers, Wellingtons and a Ventura.

On 19 September 1944 Mosquitoes attacked and sunk the *Lynx* and the *Tryirfjrd* in Askevold Fjord. FB VI 'V' of No 235 Sqn is seen here opening fire on one of the ships. Using the same tactics, on 21 October six FB VIs of Nos 235 and 248 Sqns (led by Sqn Ldr Max Guedj DSO, DFC of the latter unit), accompanied by a No 333 Sqn outrider and 15 RP firing Beaufighters, sank the 1923-ton *Eckenheim* and the 1432-ton *Vestra*, off Haugesund. One FB VI was lost in return (G A B Lord)

On 11 April a 'Tsetse' piloted by Flt Lt B C Roberts attacked a U-boat off St Nazaire while nine FB VIs of Nos 248 and 151 Sqns dealt with her four-ship escort, and a dozen Ju 88s. Roberts saw spouts of water near the

Armourers load up FB VI PZ438 of No 143 Sqn with RPs that are fitted with 25-lb warheads. When making an attack on shipping, pilots normally commenced their dive of about 45° at around 2000 ft, opened up with machine gun fire at 1500-1000 ft before using the cannons, and lastly, at about 500 ft, rocket projectiles. PZ438 joined No 143 Sqn in October 1944, and it was one of six Mosquitoes lost on 15 January 1945 in an attack on Karmoy-Marstein – it was shot down by Fw 190s at Leirvik, near Bolmo (*Charles E Brown*)

An FB VI of No 235 Sqn dramatically test-fires both RPs with 25-lb warheads and its quartet of cannon out to sea at a range at night. RPs were arranged to form a pattern spread on impact, which meant that if they were fired at the correct range, airspeed and angle of dive, four would hit the ship above the waterline and the other four would undershoot slightly to hit below the waterline. After entering the ship's hull, each would punch an 18-in hole in the far side of the vessel which allowed the sea to flood in The remains of the cordite motor would also burn inside the hull, igniting fuel and ammunition within the ship. No 235 Sqn's first RP attack occurred on 21 February 1945 (*G A B Lord*)

hull as he fired his Molins, but could claim no definite hits. Flak was again heavy and two FB VIs were downed, but two Ju 88s were claimed destroyed. A third Mosquito was lost in a crash-landing at Portreath.

In May the 'Tsetses' began attacking surface vessels in addition to U-boats, using armour-piercing shells to penetrate the wooden deck-planking of the ships in unison with rocket-firing Beaufighters that struck in shallow dives from 500 ft. On D-Day No 248 Sqn flew anti-shipping, escort and blockading sorties off the Normandy, Brittany and Biscay coasts. On 7 June two 'Tsetses', flown by Flg Offs Doug Turner DFC and Des Curtis DFC, and Flg Offs Al Bonnett, RCAF, and 'Pickles' McNicol, each made a run on a surfacing U-boat. Twelve 57 mm shells were fired at U-212, but on Bonnett's second run his cannon jammed, which

forced him to make a series of dummy dives on the U-boat – the latter crash-dived, leaving a pool of oil and a crewman on the surface. U-212 limped into St Nazaire and was repaired, but was then promptly sunk in July by Royal Navy frigates. Turner's Mosquito was hit by flak in the port wing and engine nacelle, but he and Bonnett made it back to Cornwall.

Bonnett and McNicol were killed on 9 June when Wg Cdr Tony Phillips DSO, DFC (now OC of No 248 Sqn) collided with their Mosquito whilst coming into land following a search for survivors from a German destroyer in the Channel. Phillips lost six feet of his outer wing but landed safely – he and his navigator, Flg Off R W 'Tommy' Thomson DFC, were killed on 4 July during an attack off the Brest Peninsular.

On 10 June, four No 248 Sqn Mosquitoes (led by Flt Lt S G Nunn and Flg Off J M Carlin in LR347/T) attacked U-821 with such force off Ushant that the crew abandoned ship – the U-boat was sunk by a Liberator from No 206 Sqn. That afternoon, No 248 Sqn's Flt Lt E H Jeffreys DFC and Flg Off D A Burden were downed by a motor launch carrying the survivors of U-821 during a follow up strike by two 'Tsetses' and four FB VIs. The launch was quickly sunk by the Molins cannons.

During May-June the Norwegians of No 333 Sqn also became involved in attacks on U-boats. On 26 May Lt J M Jacobsen and Sub Lt Humlen (in HR262/N), and Lts Hans Engebrightsen and Odd Jonassen, (in HP904/E) damaged U-958 in an attack off Norway – Jonassen was killed in action on 11 June when he and Engebrightsen were accidentally shot down by Spitfires. Three days later Lt Erling Johansen and 2/Lt Lauritz Humlen (in HP864/H) attacked and damaged U-290 again off Norway, putting the boat out of commission until August. On 16 June Johansen and Humlen sighted U-998 on the surface off the Norwegian coast and duly attacked with cannons blazing. Two depth charges were also dropped from 100 ft which so badly damaged the U-boat that it was paid off in Bergen harbour later that month.

On a subsequent patrol that same day, Lt Jacob M Jacobson and 2/Lt Per Hansen sighted and attacked U-804, which was also badly damaged and forced into Bergen for repairs. this vessel would later fall victim to Banff Wing Mosquitoes on 9 April 1945.

On 23 June Flt Sgts Leslie Doughty and R Grime were one of six crews from No 248 Sqn sent to patrol between Ushant and Lorient. However, they became separated from the others in bad light, but this did not stop

This FB VI is armed to the teeth, boasting four cannon, four machine guns and eight RPs (note the electrical arming 'pigtails' with Niphan plugs dangling from the rear of each 25-lb RP – these remained unplugged until engine start up time). Rocket rails had to be set so that they were parallel with the airflow at correct diving speed. If not, the RPs would weathercock, and either under or overshoot the target. This also occurred if the pilot dived at the wrong airspeed (*via GMS*)

Doughty flying on and locating a convoy of escorts and U-155, which was about to enter Lorient following her ninth patrol. The crew attacked with cannons and machine guns, and also dropped two depth charges from 50 ft. Doughty's action earned him a promotion to warrant officer and the award of the DFM. U-155 was so badly damaged in the attack that she was out of action until September, when the U-boat sailed for Norway.

Twenty-four hours earlier, wing-mounted 25-lb Mk XI depth charges and A VIII mines were used for the first time operationally by Mosqui-

FB VI RS625/NE-D of No 143 Sqn is armed with the Mk IB double tiered RP rail system, introduced in early March 1945, which allowed 100-gal under wing drop tanks to be carried in the space between the engine nacelles and the rocket rails. When operating in the tight confines of the Norwegian fjords, pilots usually had only one chance against a target so they often fired all eight RPs at once (*BAe via GMS*)

No 143 Sqn's FB VI HR405/NE-A banks away from Charles Brown's camera off the Scottish coast, exposing its rocket rails and underside details to good effect. This aircraft survived the war to eventually be struck of charge in November 1946 (*via Phil Jarrett*)

Merchantmen come under attack from marauding No 143 Sqn FB VIs in Sandshavn on 23 March 1945 (*via Phil Jarrett*)

toes. Portreath-based No 235 Sqn also flew their first FB VI sortie at this time, having completed their last Beaufighter operation on 27 June. The FB VIs flew as escort for the Beaufighters, and also intercepted Do 217s which carried Hs 293 glider bombs for attacks on Allied shipping.

BANFF STRIKE WING

Early in September 1944, Nos 235 and 248 Sqns moved to Scotland to commence operations against enemy shipping off Norway, forming the Banff Strike Wing with No 333 'Norwegian' Sqn and Nos 144 and 404 RCAF Beaufighter Sqns. The Banff Wing flew its first strike on 14 September, when 22 FB VIs, four 'Tsetses' and 19 Beaufighters sank a flak ship and a merchantman. On 28 September the Mosquitoes were modi-

fied to carry eight underwing rocket-projectiles (RPs) on rails.

At first, RPs with 60-lb semi-Armour-Piercing heads were used, but these failed to penetrate shipping and caused little structural damage. They were swiftly replaced with RPs fitted with 25-lb solid armour-piercing warheads. When attacking shipping, the Mosquitoes normally started their dive of approximately 45° at about 2000 ft, opening fire with machine guns at 1500-1000 ft, followed by cannons and, lastly, the RPs at about 500 ft. After entering the hull, each RP would punch an 18-inch hole in the far side of the vessel to allow the sea to flood in, while the remains of the

On 30 March 1945 No 235 Sqn's OC, Wg Cdr A H Simmonds, led 32 rocket-firing FB VIs (with eight more as escorts) in an attack on four merchantmen alongside at Borgestad (Porsgrunn-Skein harbour). The pall of smoke (centre) marks where the Mosquito of Flt Lt Bill Knowles and Flt Sgt L Thomas struck an overhead electric cable and crashed. Three merchantman were sunk and the fourth badly damaged, while a warehouse full of chemicals on Menstad quay was also destroyed (*via Alan Sanderson*)

cordite motor would burn inside the vessel, igniting fuel and ammunition within the ship. Mosquitoes used RPs for the first time on 26 October.

The two Beaufighter squadrons departed Banff on 24 September to form the Dallachy Wing with Nos 455 and 489 Sqns, their place being taken by No 143 Sqn, which had moved up from North Coates to convert from the Beaufighter to the Mosquito FB VI – this unit flew its first operation with the new type on 7 November. Six days later, the Banff Strike Wing and the Dallachy Wing operated in tandem for the first time. The largest operation so far took place on 21 November when 33 Mosquitoes, 42 Beaufighters and 12 Mustangs took part in a shipping strike at Aalesund. Eight days later on 29 November, Flg Off Woodcock

No 143 Sqn's FB VI HR405/NE-A is seen attacking a ship in Sandefjord harbour, in Norway, on 2 April 1945 (*via Phil Jarrett*)

FB XVIII 'Tsetse' PZ467 did not see frontline action, being sent instead to the USA on 9 April 1945 for evaluation by the US Navy at Patuxent River (*DH via Philip Birtles*)

engaged a U-boat in a diving attack off Lista, firing eight 57 mm shells and scoring two hits, while FB VIs also attacked with depth charges and cannon.

December saw several scraps with enemy fighters, seven being claimed on the 7th alone for the loss of two FB VIs, a Mustang and a Beaufighter. Attacks, meanwhile, were made on merchantmen at Ejdsfjord, Kraakhellesund and Leirvik harbour for the loss of four Mosquitoes. In January 1945 the wing made further attacks on shipping in Leirvik harbour, leaving three vessels burning and one sunk at its moorings, but losses began to rise. A second raid on the port on 15 January cost five FB VIs, including one flown by Wg Cdr Jean Maurice (pseudonym for Max Guedj DSO, DFC, CdeG), OC of No 143 Sqn. The formation had been jumped by 30 Fw 190s from III./JG 5, which also lost five fighters. Following this raid No 248 Sqn transferred to North Coates.

By March 1945 some of the Banff Wing Mosquitoes – now operating independently of the Beaufighters – had begun using tiered Mk IB RP projector rails, which permitted eight RPs *and* 50- or 100-gallon long range drop tanks to be carried on operations of increased range. On 7 March 44 Mosquitoes, escorted by 12 Mustangs, attacked eight self-propelled barges in the Kattegat with machine guns, cannon and rocket fire – two FB VIs failed to return after colliding shortly after the attack. Further raids were made that month on shipping in the Skagerrak and Kattegat, Sandshavn, Dalsfjord and Aalesund and Porsgrunn-Skein harbours. On 24 March No 404 Sqn, RCAF, began conversion from Beaufighters to FB VIs.

During April the Banff Strike Wing wreaked havoc in Norwegian waters. On the 5th 37 Mosquitoes, with two outriders from No 333 Sqn, attacked a convoy of five motor vessels and escorts in the Kattegat about three miles south of Anholt. They left every ship on fire and sinking, and an estimated 900 German troops were killed. One Mosquito hit the mast of a vessel and dived into the sea about 100 yards from its target. No 235 Sqn's RS619/LA-F, crewed by Plt Off R K Harington and Flt Sgt A E Winwood, was seen at 17.50 hours over Western Jutland leaking glycol, which forced it down in a field. This was the second time that LA-F had hit the ground during the mission, having 'bounced' off Danish soil at 280 knots after dropping into the slipstream of an aircraft ahead which was avoiding flak from vessels in Nyobing Mors harbour, in Western Jutland.

On 2 May 1945 27 Mosquitoes, led by Sqn Ldr A G Deck, sank U-2359 and damaged another *Unterseeboote*. This No 143 Sqn FB VI was photographed making its attack on the two U-boats in the Kattegat (*G A B Lord*)

Another shot of No 143 Sqn's Kattegat action on 2 May 1945 against the two U-boats – this photo shows FB VI NE-L of No 143 Sqn making a firing pass (via Alan Sanderson)

A rare shot of FB VI DM-S of No 248 Sqn, seen in flight with a large formation of Banff Wing Mosquitoes just visible on the horizon (*via Andy Bird*)

The crew left the aircraft through the top hatch to find both propellers behind them up a gentle rise, and glycol still dripping from the port nacelle – the aircraft had touched down in a flapless landing at about 140 knots. The two crew were rescued by gallant Danes, and, after many adventures, were safely conveyed to Sweden by the end of the month.

Meanwhile, on 9 April 34 Mosquitoes of Nos 248, 143 and 235 Sqns (led by Sqn Ldr H H Gunnis DFC of No 248 Sqn) came across three U-boats on the surface of the Kattegat whilst en route from Kiel to Horten. In the first action, U-804 and U-1065 were sunk through a combination of cannon fire and 70 RPs, although one of the U-boats took a photo-Mosquito with it when it exploded. Soon after, U-843 was sunk by Flg Offs A J Randell and R R Rawlins of No 235 Sqn following repeated rocket, cannon and machine gun attacks.

U-251 was sunk and two others damaged in the Kattegat on 19 April by 22 Mosquitos of the Banff Strike Wing, led by Wg Cdr A H Simmonds. Two days later 42 FB VIs of Nos 235, 248, 143 and 333 Sqns (led by Wg Cdr Foxley-Norris, OC, No 143 Sqn) shot down nine Ju 88As and Ju 188A-3 torpedo bombers of KG 26 some 150 miles off the Scottish coast. On the 22nd, No 404 'Buffalo' Sqn, RCAF, flew its first Mosquito operation from Banff, sinking a Bv 138 flying boat at its moorings.

On 2 May 27 Mosquitoes, led by Sqn Ldr A G Deck, sank U-2359 in the Kattegat and damaged a second vessel. On 4 May 48 Mosquitoes from Nos 143, 235, 248, 333 and 404 Sqns flew their last large-scale-shipping strike of the war – Flt Lt Thorburn DFC failed to return.

FB XVIII 'Tsetse' PZ468 is seen wearing the QM codes of No 254 Sqn at North Coates in June 1945. On 12 April, PZ468 had been one of five FB XVIII 'Tsetses' sent on detachment by No 248 Sqn to the Beaufighter unit at North Coates, where they were primarily used off the coast of Holland on operations against midget submarines and U-boats. Two 'Tsetses' found five U-boats on the surface on 18 April and each got off just one round apiece before the latter crash-dived. PZ468 was struck off charge on 25 November 1946 and reduced to spares (*RAF Museum via GMS*)

THE BURMA 'BRIDGE BUSTERS'

S ome of the most successful Mosquito reconnaissance operations in World War 2 were flown by aircraft based in India and the Far East, but the de Havilland 'twin' suffered so badly from problems caused by climatic conditions that many fighter-bomber units actually preferred the Beaufighter.

The first six Mosquitoes (three Mk IIs and three Mk VIs – HJ730, HJ759 and HJ760) to arrive in the Far East were delivered to India in April-May 1943. They were allocated to No 27 Sqn at Agartala as the first examples of the type to be issued to a squadron in the region. The Mk IIs were standard production aircraft sent for 'operational trials and familiarisation' only, whilst the FB VIs had been given a form of protective treatment prior to being despatched in that they had been bonded with formaldehyde glue. They were to be used for weathering trials during the forthcoming rainy season under the supervision of Mr F G Myers, de Havilland's technical representative in India. Despite the experimental nature of these aircraft, it was decided that the Mosquitoes should be used to supplement No 27 Sqn's Beaufighters on intruder missions. After a handful of operational sorties, and the loss of a Mk II in a crash, the five surviving Mosquitoes were modified for PR work and handed over to No 681 Sqn at Dum Dum, in Calcutta, in August 1943.

Two months later No 47 Sqn, which was equipped with the Beaufighter Mk X at Yelahanka, India, began receiving a few FB VIs. The 'Fly-

FB VI Series I HJ770 is seen en route to No 27 Sqn in India in late 1943. It wears standard European Dark Green/Medium Sea Grey camouflage, with 'Day fighter' markings comprising Sky spinners and fuselage band. Above the serial the word 'SNAKE' (introduced on 1 May 1943) indicated to units – especially in the Mediterranean – that the aircraft must not be diverted to other squadrons while en route to the Far East. This particular aircraft was sent to No 142 RSU following the spate of inflight structural failures, but was written off very much on the ground when a hangar roof collapsed on it at Agartala during a tropical storm on 5 May 1944 (via Geoff Thomas)

FB VI HJ811 of No 27 Sqn is seen taxying out through the aftermath of a monsoon in early 1944. Like many Series I aircraft, this aircraft was delivered in Dark Green and Ocean Grey camouflage, with Medium Sea Grey undersurfaces and 'day fighter' Sky markings. Later Mosquito fighter-bombers were repainted in the more appropriate shades of Temperate Land Scheme camouflage. HJ811 was written off in a forced landing at Rajalmundy airstrip on 1 May 1944 whilst serving with No 45 Sqn – the aircraft had suffered an engine failure on its approach to landing (*via Tom Cushing*)

Mosquitoes carried out many 'bridge busting' raids in Burma. On 19 December 1944, Wt Offs B Walsh and H Orsborn, flying HR462/J of No 45 Sqn, bombed the Saye-Kinu railway with two 500 'pounders', followed 24 hours later by a raid on the Alon railway bridge, which they successfully destroyed. These low level attacks were flown over hundreds of miles of inhospitable terrain, and were often pressed home in the face of heavy ground flak and small arms fire (*Author's Collection*)

ing Elephants" first proper Mosquito sorties were despatched on Christmas Day, and by year-end one flight had converted to the Mosquito FB VI. However, the squadron had reverted back to all-Beaufighter status once more by February 1944. The previous month the Air Ministry had decided to equip 22 bomber and strike squadrons with Mosquito FB VIs so as to replace the Vultee Vengeance and some Beaufighters – de Havilland were also contracted to produce replacement airframe components in-theatre at Karachi. No 45 Sqn duly converted onto the type at Yelahanka, near Bangalore, in February 1944, becoming the first of the Vengeance dive-bomber units to receive the Mosquito FB VI.

There then began a series of Mosquito crashes that cast great doubt over the future of the aircraft in India. On 13 May 1944 Wg Cdr Harley C Stumm DFC, RAAF, OC No 45 Sqn, and his navigator Flt Lt McKer-

Silver FB VIs of No 47 Sqn are seen in Burma in the spring of 1945. This unit began its conversion from Beaufighters to FB VIs at Yelahanka, in India, in October 1944, but structural problems with their new aircraft meant no Mosquito operations were flown, and by the end of the year the Beaufighters were back. Mosquitoes were re-introduced in February 1945, but continued problems with wooden aircraft in hot climates rendered the squadron non-operational between May and August (*Andy Thomas*)

racher, RAAF, were killed at Amarda Road when their B XXV (HP939) broke up during a practice attack. On 4 July 1944, Kolar-based No 82 Sqn and No 84 Sqn at Quetta (both bases were in India) began their conversion from the Vengeance to the FB VI. Each squadron moved in turn to Ranchi, in West Bengal, and then to Kumbhirgam, in Assam. Heavy monsoons prevented any operations at all until mid-September, and on the 13th of that month, Flg Off W C Tuproll and Flt Sgt V A Boll died when their FB VI crashed during a dummy attack on another aircraft – a glueing fault was believed to have caused the failure of the wing or tail.

No 45 Sqn flew its first Mosquito sortie on 1 October, whilst No 47 Sqn moved to Yelahanka six days later to begin conversion from Beaufighters to FB VIs. No 110 Sqn followed suit three weeks later. However, the rising spectre of structural problems meant No 47 Sqn failed to fly a single operational sortie with the Mosquito. On 4 October the wing leading edge of No 45 Sqn FB VI HX821 (flown by Sqn Ldr Norman L

FB VIs RF711/A and RF765/S of No 211 Sqn are seen at Yelahanka in early July 1945, a month after the unit had re-equipped with FB VIs. No 211 Sqn moved to Don Muang in September, but they never saw action with the Mosquito. RF711 crash-landed in the circuit at Don Muang on 31 January 1946 following an engine failure, whilst RF765 survived to be struck off charge on 30 May 1946 (*via Andy Thomas*)

A silver FB VI of No 45 Sqn is seen with its bomb bay doors still open as it leaves the target area at Yenangyaung oilfield on 15 March 1945. Some 24 Mosquitoes were involved in this mission – 12 FB VIs from No 82 Sqn went in first, attacking in a shallow-dive from 12,000 ft, followed almost immediately by a dozen more from No 45 Sqn, which approached the target in line abreast, flying flat out, over the tree tops (three FB VIs can just be seen over the trees on the far bank). Each Mosquito was carrying 11-second delayed fuse 500-lb bombs. Flak and debris (the latter included 40-gallon drums and a log) thrown up during the raid hit one of the No 45 Sqn FB VIs and forced the crew to crash-land with a hung-up bomb at the newly-built P-47 strip at Sinthe, causing much damage. Five days later the Mosquitoes returned to Yenangyaung, this time dive-bombing from high level! (*via Geoff Thomas*)

Bourke, RAAF, and Flg Off Keith Dumas, RAAF, buckled in flight, and the aircraft was duly handed over to No 143 Repair and Servicing Unit (RSU) for investigation, whereupon on 10 October the wing actually broke off at 8000 ft and the Mosquito spun in near Bishnupur, killing its crew. A subsequent investigation revealed blood and feathers at the point of impact, indicating that a large kite hawk had broken the plywood skin and caused the main spar to separate at the bad glue-joint – Bourke and Dumas were killed on 16 October following a strafing attack on Kadozeik.

On 20 October two more Mosquitoes crashed – HP919, a No 82 Sqn FB VI, shed half of its starboard wing during a practice bombing attack on Random Range, whilst HP921/O from No 45 Sqn broke up on aproach to landing at Kumbhirgram.

All 14 FB VIs of No 110 Sqn were immediately grounded by 6 November – just weeks after the last obsolescent Vengeance had been retired. It was not until January 1945 that suitable replacements enabled the squadron to re-enter frontline service just in time for the final assault on Rangoon. Mosquito operations were halted on 12 November 1944 when a signal to all units ordered all aircraft to be grounded pending inspection. The cause of the accidents was supposedly glue failure, for it was believed that within the wings of the aircraft parked in the open 'extreme heat has caused the glue to crack and the upper surface to lift from the spar'. It soon began to emerge, however, that the adhesive was not the real cause of the trouble – HP919, for example, had a 'great lack of glue', particularly along the top boom. Furthermore, it would become apparent that the problem was not confined to India.

Their Mosquitoes grounded, navigators were sent on leave and the pilots transferred to the flying ambulance unit at Cox'sBazaar, near Chittagong, to bring out wounded and sick Royal West African troops from makeshift landing strips in the Kaladan in Tiger Moths and Sentinels! No 45 Sqn's FB VIs were grounded for inspections between 1 and 18 December, before being passed airworthy and operations commencing the following day. Wt Off Ben Walsh, a pilot in the squadron at this time who made 19 recce and evacuation sorties in Moths and Sentinels, recalls;

'On 19 December my navigator, Wt Off H Orsborn, and I in HR462/J, carrying two 500-lb bombs, attacked the Saye-Kinu railway, and on the 20th the Alon railway bridge, which we successfully destroyed. These low level attacks were made over inhospitable terrain, and were often pressed home in the face of heavy ground flak and small arms fire. Meiktila aerodrome was glide-bombed with four 500-lb bombs on a night attack on the 23rd. This was followed by a 'Rhubarb' northwards from Chindwin.

'The target was revisited two days later, and at Wetlet a loco and rolling stock were shot up in a 20 mm strafing attack. Japanese flak was encountered at Sagaing. On the night of the 27th, the marshalling yards at Ywataung were bombed. On the 29th, a dawn dive-bomb attack was made on Meiktila aerodrome by six Mosquitoes. The dive-bombing technique involved approaching from around 4000 ft, and then diving to 1000 ft whilst aiming the bombs at the target. The bomb load varied between two 500-lb and four 500-lb loads, and we often carried instantaneous fused bombs, which gave little margin for error. The Japs put up a large amount of heavy flak as we attacked the airfield. Flying HR456/M, we were intercepted by six "Oscars", and in the ensuing melee, I managed to get a prolonged cannon and machine gun shot at one and I believe I damaged it. However, we could not get confirmation, since I was the last of our six Mossies in the attack. All Mosquitoes got back safely.

'From 3 January 1945 onwards, it was a time of intense operational activity, even though the weather was often totally unhelpful because of

FB Mk 40 A52-41 of the Royal Australian Air Force's No 94 Sqn. The second RAAF-controlled unit to receive the Mosquito during World War 2, No 94 Sqn was formed at Castlereagh, in New South Wales (NSW), in May 1945, but it never flew its locally-built fighter-bombers in action – in fact it operated them for just four months. Indeed, the only RAAF attack unit to engage the enemy with the aircraft in the Far East was No 1 Sqn, who were part of No 86 Wing within the 1st Tactical Air Force. This unit began exchanging its Beaufighters for imported FB VIs at Kingaroy, in Queensland, in January 1945, and a detachment of two aircraft was sent to Morotai to familiarise the USAAF and local RAAF units with the Mosquito two months later. It was not until early August that the whole unit went into action, flying its first sortie from Labuan Island on the 7th of the month. Between then and 15 August, when hostilities ceased, No 1 Sqn completed a total of 65 sorties against all manner of ground targets. This particular Mosquito was initially used by No 5 OTU at Williamtown, NSW, in late 1944, before it was rebuilt as a Mk 41 and reserialled A52-321 in March 1948. It was eventually sold into private hand exactly a decade later (*BAe via GMS*)

Built by Standard Motors in Coventry as HR502 in late 1944, this aircraft (A52-500) was shipped to Australia as the first of 38 FB VIs supplied directly to the RAAF in order to re-equip No 1 Sqn following production line difficulties with locally-manufactured Mosquitoes. It survived with the unit until August 1945, when it crashed during take-off at Labuan and was written off (*via Phil Jarrett*)

the small monsoons. Jap airfields – especially Meiktila – were the primary targets for low level bombing, strafing and night patrols. Road communication, railways and bridges got their fair share of attention too. On 8 January, whilst flying with Wt Off S M D Nessim, we made a dive-bomb ing attack on Jap troop concentrations at Sagaing. Four days later we paired up with Wt Off H Orsborn on a "Rhubarb" to Chindwin and along the Irrawaddy to Sagaing – Jap installations at Konywa waterfront were bombed. A further ten ops were flown during the month – MT transport, railway installations, bullock carts and sampans were all bombed and strafed. On the 16th we flew a dawn strike on Meiktila and a "Rhubarb" on the Irrawaddy-Chank road. Jap ground fire hit our starboard spinner and main spar close to the starboard radiator, and although the outer fuel tanks were damaged, we completed the op safely. A later inspection of HR409/D revealed that the damage was superficial.

'On 18 January the Jap HQ at Kokko was hit with four 500-lb bombs, and the following night river traffic was shot up between Sagaing and Yenang Yaung. We were despatched on a night attack on the 23rd to bomb either Heho airfield or Meiktila, but the weather was "duff" so we dive-bombed Myingyan with five 500 "pounders" fitted with instantaneous fuses instead. The round trip took 4 hours and 20 minutes to complete. On the 26th a daylight attack was made on petrol dumps in Port Duffern, and three MTs were shot up on the Mandalay road. On take-off the next day, HR547/H developed a hydraulics fault and the op had to be aborted. On the 29th a night attack was made on the Myitinge bridge by

12 Mosquitoes. A considerable amount of flak was put up, and this burst uncomfortably close to the aircraft. Jap stores at Ywabop were bombed on the 31st and transport was attacked along the Irrawaddy-Myingyan-Magwe road and railway. Some Jap ground fire hit the Mossie in the fuselage during this part of the operation.'

The effects of the accidents in India, meanwhile, were far-reaching. A meeting at the Air Ministry in London on 1 January 1945 heard an explanation of the Mosquito defects from Maj Hereward de Havilland, who had led an investigative team to India.. Despite the gluing problems, the Air Ministry preferred to believe the major's assertion that the accidents were caused by 'faults largely due to climate', or 'loss of control'. In India, Mosquitoes found to have skin defects caused by the use of casein glue were simply struck off charge, while precautions were taken to prevent further losses to existing aircraft. An inspection panel was added at the main spar joint, and all aircraft were stripped of their camouflage and repainted silver to reduce the temperature inside the wing by about 15°C.

The absence of camouflage made the Mosquitoes much more conspicuous, however, especially on low level bombing operations. Re-equipment of the Beaufighter squadron proceeded slowly, and during February 1945 No 89 Sqn, at Baigachi, began converting to the FB VI, but they were never used operationally. Yelahanka-based No 211 Sqn started re-equipping with FB VIs in June 1945, and moved to Don Maung in September, but they too saw no action with the Mosquito. Despite completing their conversion onto the FB VI in March 1945, No 84 Sqn also failed to see action against the Japanese.

No 45 Sqn, meanwhile, continued their punishing schedule of FB VI operations, as Wt Off Ben Walsh recalls;

'On 10 February four of us were sent out on an operation over a 8000-10,000 ft mountain range for Army support to drop two one- and two-hour delayed "Parafex" ("Canned Battle") containers (simulating hand grenades, mortar shells, machine gun and rifle fire) in a predetermined spot on the east bank of the Irrawaddy between Chauk and Yenangyaung to assist in an army crossing. Near the target HR567 experienced a total electrics failure, and believing we had dropped the "Parafex" on target, we endeavoured to make our way back to base without a radio.

'Needless to say, with no moon, flooding and swollen rivers, and increasing high cumulus, especially over the mountains, we got hope-

FB VI HR551 of No 82 Sqn is seen at Cholavaram, Madras, in mid-1945. Mosquitoes found to have skin defects caused by the use of casein glue were simply struck off charge, while precautions were taken to prevent further losses to existing Mosquitoes. An inspection panel was added at the main spar joint and all aircraft were stripped of their camouflage and resprayed silver in an effort to reduce the heat absorption of the airframe. This Mosquito was eventually struck off charge in October 1946 (L Bradford via Geoff Thomas)

No 82 Sqn's RF784/UX-N is seen from a second Mosquito FB VI on a sortie from Kumbhirgram in early 1945. This aircraft also served with No 47 Sqn for a time, before being struck off charge in October 1946 (*via Phil Jarrett*)

lessly lost and were very low on fuel. We were almost at the point of bailing out when, by a sheer stroke of luck, we spotted the lights of a very small strip and made an emergency landing (downwind as it happened). The plane overshot the lights and ploughed through a burnt out DC-3 and was badly damaged, and because of the electrics failure, we found the "Parafex" was also still on board! This forward landing strip was Onbauk, near Mandalay, and the Jap ground forces were all around it, often attacking at night with mortar and machine gun fire. The next morning we got a transport to Imphal and then back to base.

'Between 5-31 March, No 45 Sqn kept up a relentless and intense bombing and strafing campaign against the Japs in Burma. Road and rail transport was shot up at every opportunity, and bridges at Thamakan (missed), Thwatti (badly damaged), Sinthe (damaged) and Toungoo, were bombed. One of the best results was obtained on 26/27 March when Salin was bombed at first light – four 500-lb bombs were dropped accurately on a Jap camp. The following day, a "Rhubarb" was carried out on the railway and road between Kyaukpadauna-Pyinmana. Two locos were shot up and a three-ton MT set alight before the ammunition ran out!'

On 15 March Flg Off Don Blenkhorne and Wt Off Alf Pridmore took off in HJ368 at 11.20 hours for Yenanyang oilfield. Pridmore recalls;

'No 45 Sqn approached the target line abreast, flying flat out over the tree tops. Each aircraft carried short delay bombs, and we released ours in

HR559/UX-X was also on strength with No 82 Sqn at the same time as the Mosquito featured at the top of this page. Prior to serving with this unit, the FB VI had spent a short time with No 1 Ferry Unit. Like RF784, this Mosquito was withdrawn from service in October 1946 following No 82 Sqn's transition to Spitfire PR 19s and Lancaster PR 1s (*via Phil Jarrett*)

B Mk XXV TA272 is pictured at the end of the war in silver overall, with Dull Blue bands and codes. The actual squadron allocation of this particular aircraft remains unclear, but it was struck off charge in September 1946 (*Author's Collection*)

the target area and then headed home. The Japs put up a moderate amount of flak but did no damage. The operation lasted 3 hours 20 minutes. Two days later the squadron returned to the target area, bombing this time from high level. The load carried was usually two bombs in the bomb bay and two more under the wings if drop tanks were not needed. Attacks on airfields could be dangerous, but they were necessary as it was important to try and keep the Jap aircraft on the ground. In March, these operations were often carried out at night or timed for dawn, but in May we carried out "cab rank" operations to keep a constant patrol over an airfield to prevent aircraft from taking off. Unfortunately this did not prevent the Japs from calling up aircraft from other fields, and we did suffer some losses. However, we must have been lucky for we never met a Jap aircraft, and any damage was usually the result of ground fire.'

Wt Offs Walsh and Orsborn's 40th, and final, operation on the afternoon of 4 April 1945 nearly ended in disaster. They took off in HR567/F for the advanced landing ground at Thazi, en route to Zinga. After an hour they landed to refuel, taking off again on the final 1 hour 40 minute flight to the target. On board were two 500-lb bombs and two 500-lb

FB VIs of No 211 Sqn are seen lined up at either Yelahanka or St Thomas Mount in July 1945. The aircraft nearest the camera is RF751/B, which was struck off charge in February 1946 (*via Geoff Thomas*)

Armourers clean out the cannon barrels of a Mosquito FB VI at Labuan, in Borneo. Late in 1945, Nos 47, 82, 84 and 110 Sqns carried out low level bombing and rocket attacks on Indonesian separatists in the Dutch East Indies, until more faulty wing structures were discovered in a number of FB VIs and the Mosquito force was briefly grounded once again for inspection (*via Ron Mackay*)

incendiaries. As the evening light faded they ran in to bomb Zinga village, and as they left the target, it appeared that it had been accurately hit.

The return trip took three hours in the dark, and after a time it became apparent that the fuel situation was not good. Estimates indicated that there would be insufficient fuel to enable the aircraft to reach base, so Walsh called for an emergency homing to Monywa. Insufficient flares were laid at the strip and the Mosquito overshot, having made a final approach from 5000 ft with very little fuel left. It crashed through a gun position, leaving HR567 a 'write off', but the crew sustained no injuries.

Mosquitoes continued to harry the Japanese until the surrender. On 12 August No 47 Sqn flew its last wartime sortie before its Mosquitoes were taken out of service to have RP rails fitted, whilst two days later Wg Cdr A E Saunders, OC No 110 Sqn, and Flt Lt Stephens actually took the final surrender of Rangoon. Having dropped the first RAF bombs of the war when flying Blenheim IVs, No 110 Sqn also rather fittingly dropped the last bombs of World War 2 on 20 August 1945, when eight FB VIs were used to dislodge Japanese troops at Tikedo, east of the Sittang river, who had refused to surrender. It was the final RAF operation of the war. On 3 September Gen Itazaki, the Japanese Southern Area Commander, formerly surrendered to Vice-Admiral Lord Louis Mountbatten in Singapore, thus bringing the conflict with Japan to an end.

Late in 1945, Nos 47, 82, 84 and 110 Sqns, based at Labaun, in Borneo, carried out low level bombing and rocket attacks on Indonesian separatists in the Dutch East Indies, until more faulty wing-structures were discovered in some FB VIs and they were briefly grounded for inspection once again.

Armourers finish loading bombs aboard a FB VI destined to attack Indonesian separatists in Borneo in December 1945 (*via Ron Mackay*)

APPENDICES

MOSQUITO BOMBER AND FIGHTER-BOMBER SQUADRONS

21 (YH)	140 Wing, 2 Group, 2nd TAF	1655 MTU	8 Group (PFF)
464 RAAF (SB)	140 Wing, 2 Group, 2nd TAF	617 (AJ)	5 Group, Bomber Command
487 RNZAF (EG)	140 Wing, 2 Group, 2nd TAF	618 (OP)	No 18 Group, Coastal Command
107 (OM)	138 Wing, 2 Group, 2nd TAF	143 (NE)	Banff Strike Wing*
305 (SM)	138 Wing, 2 Group, 2nd TAF	235 (LA)	Banff Strike Wing*
613 (SY)	138 Wing, 2 Group, 2nd TAF	248 (DM/WR)	Banff Strike Wing*
105 (PFF) (GB)	2 Group/8 Group (PFF) (from 5/43)	333 RNWAF (KK)	Banff Strike Wing*
109 (PFF) (HS)	2 Group/8 Group (PFF) (from 1/6/43)	334 RNWAF (VB)	Banff Strike Wing*
128 (M5)	8 Group (PFF)	404 RCAF (EO)	Banff Strike Wing*
139 (PFF) (XD)	2 Group/8 Group (PFF) (From 5/43)	489 RNZAF (P6)	Banff Strike Wing*
142 (4H)	8 Group (PFF)	45 (OB)	India
162 (CR)	8 Group (PFF)	47 (KU)	India
163	8 Group (PFF)	82 (UX)	India
571 (8K)	8 Group (PFF)	84 (PY)	India
608 (6T/RAO)	8 Group (PFF)	110 (VE)	India
627 (AZ)	8 Group (PFF)/5 Group (from 13/4/44)	211	India
692 (P3)	8 Group (PFF)	1 RAAF (NA)	Borneo
1409 Met Flt (AE)	8 Group (PFF)		(*Formed, 9/44)

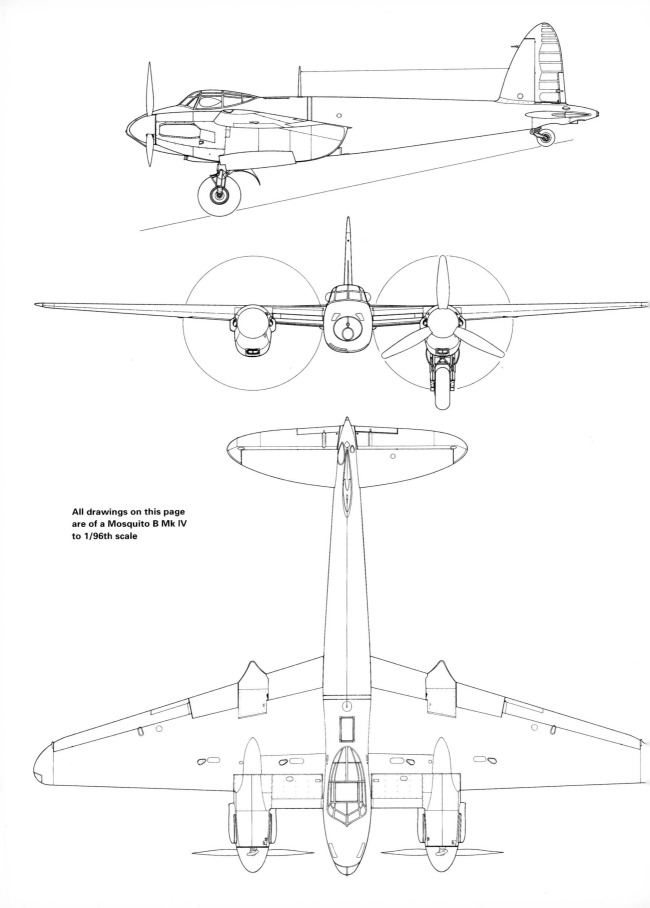

**All drawings on this page
are of a Mosquito B Mk IV
to 1/96th scale**

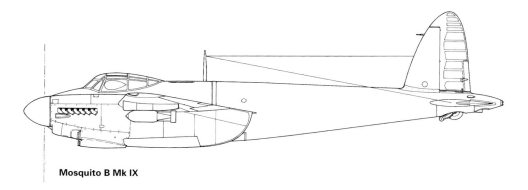

Mosquito B Mk IX

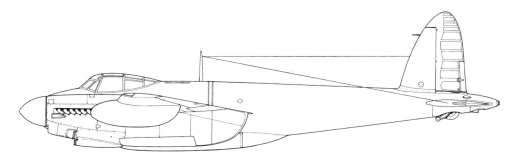

Mosquito B Mk XVI

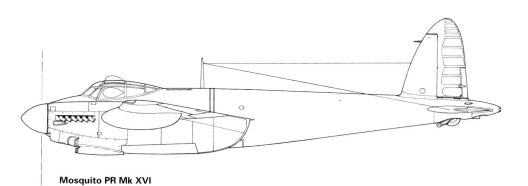

Mosquito PR Mk XVI

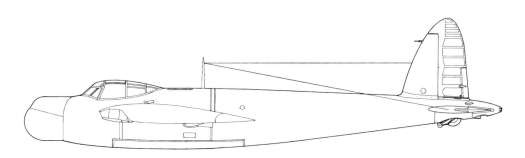

**Mosquito B Mk XVI
(radar nose)**

COLOUR PLATES

1

B Mk IV Series II DK296/GB-G of No 105 Sqn, No 2 Group, flown by Flt Lt D A G 'George' Parry DFC and Flg Off V Robson, 1/2 June 1942

Highly-polished for extra speed, DK296 made its operational debut on 1/2 June 1942 in the wake of the 'Thousand Bomber' raid on Cologne. On 11 July 'G-George' was badly damaged when Sgt P W R Rowland flew so low on the raid on Flensburg that he hit a roof and returned with pieces of chimney pot lodged in the aircraft's nose. On 25 September Parry and Robson used DK296 to lead an attack by four Mosquitoes on the Gestapo HQ in Oslo. 'G-George' was then passed on to Sqn Ldr Bill Blessing DSO, DFC, RAAF, who crash-landed it at Marham and broke its back. The aircraft was duly repaired, and on 24 August 1943 was placed in store with No 10 MU at Hullavington. The following month it was issued to No 305 Ferry Training Unit at Errol, in Scotland, where it was given Red Air Force markings and used to train Soviet crews who were converting onto Albermarles. On 20 April 1944 DK296 was ferried to the Soviet Union by a Russian crew, being officially accepted on 31 August 1944 and subsequently serving with the Red Air Force. Its ultimate fate is unknown.

2

B Mk IV Series II DK301, No 105 Sqn, flown by Flt Lt D A G Parry and Flg Off V Robson, August 1942

Stripped of its camouflage scheme, codes, serial, and national insignia, and painted overall pale grey, this aircraft was used by Parry and Robson for the first Mosquito diplomatic run to Stockholm, via Leuchars, on 4 August 1942, the crew delivering mail and cyphers for the British Embassy. Whilst airborne on a training flight on 8 November 1942, pilot Flt Sgt N Booth was unable to lower the undercarriage and DK301 belly-landed in a field at Abbey Farm, near RAF Marham. The aircraft was struck off charge (SoC) nine days later.

3

B Mk IV Series II DZ414/O of the FPU, flown by Flt Lt C E S Patterson, 14 February 1943

This aircraft was picked out at Hatfield on 22 December 1942 by Flt Lt C E S Patterson for service with the FPU. He subsequently flew DZ414 for 20,000 of its 24,000 miles, including its debut operation to Lorient on 14 February 1943 in the wake of the 466-bomber raid staged the night before, the night bombing attack on Berlin on 20/21 April 1943 (performed to coincide with Hitler's birthday), when DZ414 was badly damaged by flak, the raids on Turin and Nürnburg, and on the long-range operation to Jena on 27 May. The second 'B' on the nose is for the Berlin operation on 13/14 May 1943. Whilst part of the 2nd TAF, DZ414 took part in many notable operations, including 14 anti-*Diver* sorties flown by Flt Lt Vic Hester of No 613 Sqn, along with cameraman, Flg Off Oakley, between 19-25 June 1944. The aircraft also participated in the Amiens prison raid on 18 February 1944, its pilot Flt Lt Tony Wickham, making three passes over the burning prison so as to allow Plt Off Leigh Howard to film the flight of 255 of the 700 prisoners released through the breached walls. Finally, on 21 March 1945 DZ414 was flown by Flt Lt K L Greenwood of No 487 Sqn, RNZAF, as part of the force sent on the Shellhaus raid, Flg Off E Moore of the FPU filming the first wave attack on the building. Despite is wartime contribution, this veteran machine was SoC in October 1946 and unceremoniously scrapped.

4

B Mk IV DZ476/XD-S of No 139 Sqn, flown by Flt Lt G S W Rennie, RCAF, and Flg Off W Embry, RCAF, 4 March 1943

This Canadian pair flew as one of the 'shallow diver' crews on raids to the railway engine sheds at Aulnoye on 4 March 1943 (a flak burst during this trip hit the fuselage and severed the rudder control cables), to the John Cockerill Steel and Armament Works at Liége on 12 March, and to the engine sheds at Paderborn four days later. In April 1943, Rennie and Embry were one of eleven crews posted from Marham to Skitten to form 'A' Flight within the newly-created No 618 Sqn – they finished their tour and returned to Canada on 8 August 1944. DZ476 remained with No 139 Sqn until it was lost in a crash at Upwood on 1 January 1944.

5

B Mk IV Series II DZ601/AZ-A, No 627 Sqn, No 5 Group, flown by Flg Off J F Thomson DFC, RNZAF, and Flg Off B E B Harris, Woodhall Spa, May 1944

Prior to its arrival at No 627 Sqn, this aircraft had been used by Wg Cdr Reg W Reynolds DSO*, DFC, OC of No 139 Sqn, and his navigator, Flg Off Ted Sismore, for the raid on the Schott Glass Works at Jena on 27 May 1943 – it had suffered flak damage to its port engine propeller blade during the operation. DZ601 had been assigned to No 139 Sqn on 17 May 1943, and first saw action some ten days later. On 24 May 1944 it was issued to No 627 Sqn at Woodhall Spa, where it became AZ-A. On 28 May 1944, whilst crewed by Flg Offs J F Thomson DFC, RNZAF, and B E B Harris, DZ601 was one of four Mosquitoes to drop TIs on the gun batteries at St Martin de Varreville for Lancasters of No 5 Group. Three days later, after returning from a raid on the Saumur marshalling yards, Thomson and Harris had to belly-land DZ601 after its port engine over-revved and would not feather. Although the aircraft was repaired, it flew no more operational sorties prior to being SoC on 16 October 1946.

6

B Mk IV DZ421 Series II/XD-G of No 139 Sqn, flown by the OC, Wg Cdr Peter Shand and Plt Off C D Handley DFM, Marham, early 1943

Shand and Handley flew this aircraft regularly until they were shot down and killed over Berlin in DZ386 by Oberleutnant Lothar Linke of IV./NJG 1 on the night of 20/21 April 1943. DZ421 was transferred to No 627 Sqn on 21 April 1944, where it was re-coded AZ-C. Like DZ601, this aircraft also participated in the St Martin de Varreville operation, its crew on this occasion being Flt Lts R L Bartley DFC and J O Mitchell, RCAF. Sent for repairs soon after this raid, DZ421 then went to No 1655 Mosquito Training Unit, where it was lost on 25 July 1944 when it broke up in flight over Acklam, in Yorkshire, before crashing at Wistrow.

7

B Mk IX *Oboe* LR507/GB-F of No 109 Sqn, No 8 Group (PFF), Wyton, 17 June 1943

This aircraft served with No 109 Sqn for just 18 days between 17 June and 5 July 1943, when it was reassigned to No 105 Sqn. Paired up with LR506 for its first mission (flown on 13/14 July), LR507 carried out a diversionary operation dropping TIs over Cologne for the Main Force attack on Aachen. On 10/11 April 1944, LR507 (and RV322) dropped TIs for the first of three waves of Mosquitoes involved in a 77-aircraft strong raid on Berlin. On 21 September 1945 LR507 was delivered to No 22 MU, and was finally SoC on 15 May 1946.

8

B Mk XVI ML942/P3-D of No 692 Sqn, No 8 Group (PFF), Graveley, March 1944

This aircraft spent its entire career in No 8 Group (PFF), being delivered firstly to No 1409 Met Flight on 29 January 1944, then assigned to No 139 Sqn on 4 February, before moving onto No 692 Sqn at Graveley on 13 March. Early in April 1944, ML942 joined No 571 Sqn working up at Graveley, and was one of two aircraft (the other being ML963) to undertake the first squadron operation on 12/13 April 1944. Sent to bomb Osnabruck with a single 4000-lb 'Cookie', the aircraft was crewed by squadron OC, Wg Cdr J M Birkin DSO, DFC, AFC, and Flt Lt Saunders. ML942 completed 91 operations and suffered two aborts with No 571 Sqn before it failed to return from a raid on Berlin

on 5/6 January 1945. Flown on this occasion by Flg Offs F Henry and 'Blue' Stinson, 'D-Dog' was hit by flak in the starboard wing and engine during its bombing run. Henry managed to nurse it as far as the Belgian-French border, where it entered a spin and both crew were forced to bale out.

9

B Mk IV DZ637/AZ-X of No 627 Sqn, No 5 Group, flown by Flg Off Ronnie F Pate and Flt Lt Edward A Jackson, Woodhall Spa, 3 July 1944

This Mosquito was one of 20 modified by Marshalls and Vickers-Armstrongs in 1944 so as to allow it to carry a 4000-lb bomb. Delivered to No 627 Sqn, within No 5 Group, at Woodhall Spa on 3 July 1944, it participated in the 12-aircraft raid on the Gestapo HQ in Oslo on 31 December 1944. Crewed by Flg Off Ronnie F Pate and Flt Lt Edward A Jackson, it was one of six B Mk IVs that comprised 'Blue Force' in the second wave. Although the first wave dive-bombed the target, none of the 'Blue Force' Mosquitoes dropped their ordnance because smoke obscured the target – they had been ordered not to bomb unless they could see the HQ building. DZ637 was shot down over Siegen on 1 February 1945, with the loss of Flt Lt R Baker, RCAF, and Sgt D G Betts.

10

B Mk XXV KB416/AZ-P of No 627 Sqn, No 5 Group, flown by Wg Cdr G W Curry DFC with Flt L K G Tice, Woodhall Spa, 31 December 1944

Built in Canada (and powered by Merlin 225 engines), this aircraft was one of 343 allocated to Britain from 6 July 1944 onwards. KB416 was assigned to No 627 Sqn at Woodhall Spa on 20 October 1944, and on 31 December it led the 'Red Force' attack on the Gestapo HQ at Oslo. Flown by Wg Cdr G W Curry DFC and Flt Lt K G Tice, the crew dive-bombed from 1300 ft at an angle of 30° and hit the north-east corner of the building. On 3 July 1945 KB416 crashed whilst trying to land at Woodhall Spa on one engine – its pilot, Flt Lt D N Johnson, was killed in the subsequent blaze, and his navigator, Plt Off J D Finlayson, injured. The latter's rescuer, Cpl Stephen Cogger, was awarded the George Medal for his bravery.

11

B Mk XXV KB462/CR-B of No 162 Sqn, Bourn, December 1944

Initially issued to No 142 Sqn at Gransden Lodge on 14 November 1944, this aircraft was re-assigned to No 162 Sqn at Bourn on 17 December. It rejoined its original unit on 30 April 1945, before being assigned to No 627 Sqn at Woodhall Spa on 14 August 1945, who flew it until they disbanded on 1 October 1945 – the unit was renumbered No

109 Sqn on the same day. KB462 finished its career with this unit, being SoC on 22 October 1947.

12

B Mk XVI MM138/P3-A *Moncton Express III* of No 692 Sqn, No 8 Group (PFF), flown by Flt Lt Andy Lockhart DFC, RCAF, and Flt Lt Ralph Wood DFC, RCAF, Graveley, October 1944

The third, and last, aircraft to bear this name, MM138 was predominantly the mount of Flt Lts Andy Lockhart DFC, RCAF and F/L Ralph Wood DFC, RCAF during their tour of 50 operations, flown between 6 July and 3/4 November 1944. The first *Moncton Express* (P3-J), which the crew named after their 13th trip, to Hanover, on 13 August, was very badly damaged by cannon fire later that month whilst being flown by another crew. Lockhart and Wood used *Moncton Express II* (P3-A) for the first time on 8 September, when they flew her to Nuremburg at 29,000 ft laden down with a 'Cookie'. This aircraft was lost while they were on leave, and *Moncton Express III* made its debut on 29/30 September when they went to Karlsruhe. It was also the mount for their final sortie, which saw them visit Berlin for the 17th time.

13

B Mk IV Series II *Oboe* marker DK333/HS-F *Grim Reaper* of No 109 Sqn, No 8 Group (PFF), flown by Flg Offs Harry B Stephens and Frank R Ruskell DFC, Wyton, January 1943

On 27 January 1943 DK333 was one of three Mosquitoes to drop the first ground target indicators (250-lb marker bombs) in action. In 1944 Flg Offs Harry B Stephens and Frank Ruskell DFC flew DK333 during their tour, the latter leaving No 109 Sqn in April 1944 whilst the former was later killed in action. DK333 also served with Nos 105, 139 and 192 Sqns, before being SoC on 30 May 1945.

14

B Mk IV Series II DZ650/P3-L of No 692 Sqn, No 8 Group (PFF), Graveley, May 1944

B Mk IV Series II DZ650, whose bomb bay was strengthened and the bomb doors re-designed to carry a 4000-lb bomb, was delivered to No 692 Sqn (the first Mosquito unit to drop a 4000-lb bomb over Germany) at Bourn on 15 May 1944. P3-L flew its first operation on 28/29 May 1944, and was allocated to No 627 Sqn at Woodhall Spa on 27 July 1944, where it became AZ-Q. On 29 December 1944 DZ650 was one of eight Mosquitoes detailed to carry out 'Gardening' (minelaying) operations in the Elbe, but it was damaged beyond repair during a take-off crash at the start of this mission.

15

B Mk XVI ML963/8K-K, No 692 Sqn, flown by Flg

Off R Oliver and Flt Sgt M Young, April 1945

Originally assigned to No 109 Sqn on 9 March 1944, this aircraft was then transferred to No 692 Sqn on 24 March, before finally arriving at No 571 Sqn on 12 April – 'K-King' performed the latter unit's premier sortie on 12/13 April 1944. Between 20-24 March 1945, ML963 (now coded 'F-Freddie') flew six consecutive operations to Berlin. It was finally lost on a yet another flight to Berlin on 10/11 April (ML963's 87th mission) when it suffered an engine fire. Having firstly jettisoned their 4000-lb bomb, Flg Off Richard Oliver and Flt Sgt Max Young successfully baled out near the Elbe.

16

B Mk IV DZ383/? of No 138 Wing, 2nd TAF, Lasham, September 1944

This aircraft was known as 'the query' because it did not belong to any single unit within the three squadrons that comprised No 138 Wing, 2nd TAF, at Lasham, in Hampshire, in 1943-44. A Polish airman's first attempt to paint a question mark on DZ383 went awry as he got it the wrong way round on one side! On 17 September 1944, DZ383 was flown by Flt Lt Vic A Hester of No 613 Sqn whilst cameraman Flg Off Ted Moore filmed firstly the attack on a barracks at Arnhem ahead of the *Market Garden* operation, then the actual airborne drop itself. During the Shellhaus raid on 21 March 1945, DZ383 was flown by Flg Off R E 'Bob' Kirkpatrick, an American pilot with No 21 Sqn, accompanied by cameraman Sgt R Hearne from No 4 FPU. Although the Mosquito was damaged by flak over Copenhagen, Kirkpatrick nursed 'the query' back to Norfolk, where he force-landed at the USAAF B-24 base at Rackheath, near Norwich.

17

FB VI MM404/SB-T of No 464 Sqn, RAAF, No 140 Wing, 2nd TAF, flown by Sqn Ldr Ian McRitchie, RAAF, and Flt Lt R W 'Sammy' Sampson, 18 February 1944

Flown on the Amiens Prison raid on 18 February 1944, MM404 was hit by flak and crash-landed by a badly wounded McRitchie at over 200 mph, near Poix. He was made PoW, but his navigator, 'Sammy' Sampson, was killed.

18

FB VI MM417/EG-T of No 487 Sqn, RNZAF, No 140 Wing, No 2 Group, 2nd TAF, late February 1944

This aircraft suffered flak damage whilst attacking a *Noball* site at Le Haye, west of Carentan, in France, on 26 March 1944, and was written off in the subsequent crash-landing at its Hunsdon base.

19

FB VI MM403/SB-V of No 464 Sqn, RAAF, No 140

Wing, No 2 Group, 2nd TAF, 18 February 1944

Also on the Amiens raid, this FB VI was crewed by Flt Lts Tom McPhee and Geoffrey W Atkins. It was one of five aircraft from the unit (along with the FB VI of Grp Capt Percy Pickard) that, between them, breached the walls of the main building and destroyed the guards' quarters at the eastern and western ends of the jail. MM403 was lost in action near Merville on 18 January 1945.

20

FB VI HX917/EG-E of No 487 Sqn, RNZAF, Hunsdon, July 1943

No 487 Sqn was part of the famous No 140 Wing which carried out a number of pin-point raids on German high-security targets in 1944-45. HX917 was lost on a night mission on 5 July 1944.

21

FB VI LR366/SY-L of No 613 Sqn, No 138 Wing, 2nd TAF, Lasham, January 1944

LR366 was assigned to this unit as on 10 January 1944, and was damaged on 5 February during a raid on a *Noball* site at Motteville. Assigned to No 107 Sqn on 27 July 1944 as OM-L, LR366 was lost on 17 September 1944 when 32 FB VIs of Nos 107 and 613 Sqn attacked the barracks at Arnhem ahead of the *Market Garden* airborne invasion.

22

FB VI PZ306/YH-Y of No 21 Sqn, No 140 Wing, No 2 Group, 2nd TAF, flown by Sqn Ldr A F Carlisle DFC and Flt Lt N J Ingram, RNZAF, 21 March 1945

The crew of this FB VI flew as deputy lead in the first wave on the Shellhaus raid on 21 March 1945 behind Grp Capt Bob Bateson and Sqn Ldr Ted Sismore. Carlisle bombed the Gestapo HQ building, seeing his bombs explode at street level, and then attacked a train in Jutland on the way home.

23

B Mk IV Series II DK290/G *Highball*, A&AEE Boscombe Down, April 1943

This aircraft was used extensively during the *Highball* trials both with and without the two dummy stores (wooden-skinned bombs), which were installed at Heston. It was dived at full throttle to 390 mph ASI, during which the test pilot had to use maximum force to hold the aircraft in the dive – this force was only slightly less when the aircraft was dived without stores. At one time DK290/G (the 'G' denoted that a permanent guard had to be maintained when not flying) sported a polished finish and wing root fillets. Stability tests were made with a 10° diahedral tailplane. No 618 Sqn was later equipped with *Highball* Mosquitoes, although the bombs were never dropped in anger. DK290/G saw its final service as instructional

airframe 4411M, assigned to No 10 School of Technical Training at Kirkam, in Lancashire.

24

FB VI HR405/NE-A, No 143 Sqn, Banff Strike Wing, flown by Flg Offs A V Randell and R R Rawlins

Part of an order for 500 FB VIs built by Standard Motors Ltd of Coventry between June 1943 and December 1944, little is known about the frontline service career of this aircraft.

25

FB VI LR347/T of No 248 Sqn, Banff Strike Wing, flown by Flt Lt Stanley G Nunn and Flg Off J M Carlin, 10 June 1944

This aircraft was used by Nunn and Carlin to attack Type VIIC U-boat U-821, commanded by Oberleutnant Ulrich Knacfuss, off Ushant on 10 June 1944, the vessel eventually being sunk by Liberator EV943/K of No 206 Sqn. In July 1944 'T-Tommy' made a belly landing at Portreath after suffering flak damage which knocked out its port engine. The aircraft was repaired and later served with No 8 OTU, before being SoC in August 1946.

26

FB VI/Mk XVIII NT225/O of No 248 Sqn, Banff Wing, June 1944

Built as an FB VI at Hatfield in early 1944 and then converted into a Mk XVIII prior to delivery to No 248 Sqn at Banff on 5 June 1944, NT225 was one of two 'Tsetses' (the other was NT224/E) lost on 7 December 1944. Some 21 Mosquitoes and 40 Beaufighters, escorted by 12 Mustangs, had set out to attack a convoy in Aalesund harbour, but as landfall was made as briefed, Sqn Ldr Barnes DFC led them further up the coast towards Gossen airfield, whereupon they were jumped by about 25 Fw 190s and Bf 109Gs – Mustangs shot down four fighters and two more collided. The two 'Tsetses' were flown by Bill Cosman and K C Wing.

27

FB XVIII PZ468/QM-D of No 248 Sqn, North Coates, April 1945

This aircraft was one of five 'Tsetses' sent on detachment to Beaufighter-equipped No 254 Sqn at North Coates on 12 April 1945. Here, they were used primarily on operations off the coast of Holland against midget submarines and U-boats, with Spitfire Mk XIVs providing fighter cover. Two 'Tsetses' found five U-boats on the surface on 18 April 1945, and each got off just one round apiece before the submarines crash-dived. PZ468 was SoC on 25 November 1946 and reduced to spares.

28

FB VI RF610/DM-H, No 248 Sqn, Banff, April 1945

Built by Standard Motors Ltd of Coventry, this aircraft was delivered to No 248 Sqn at Banff in April 1945. Placed in storage after the unit disbanded in October 1946, RF610 was allocated to the French Government in April 1948, but this was rescinded and in July the aircraft was put to use at the Armament Practice Station at Acklington. In October 1949, after a further spell in storage with No 22 MU, the aircraft was flown to No 10 Ferry Unit at Abingdon for delivery (as '8114') to the Yugoslav Air Force on 10 September 1952.

29
FB VI A52-504 (ex-HR335)/NA-P of No 1 Sqn, RAAF, Labuan Island, July 1945
Built by Standard Motors Ltd, this aircraft was amongst the first batch of ten British-built FB VIs to arrive in Australia in November 1944. A total of 38 were sent out in order to offset the delays caused by problems with the local production line – the last of these aircraft arrived in April 1945. A52-504 experienced the briefest taste of combat against the Japanese during No 1 Sqn's eight days in action. It was put up for disposal in July 1949.

30
FB VI HR402/OB-C of No 45 Sqn, flown by Flt Lt C R Goodwin and Flg Off S Potts, Kumbhirgram, 15 January 1945
This Mosquito was assigned to No 45 Sqn at Kumbhirgram, in India, on 11 December 1944 as OB-C. It is painted in full Air Command South-East Asia (ACSEA) colours of green/dark earth camouflage, with national markings in light and dark blue. On 15 January 1945 HR402 was shot down by Ki-43 'Oscars' while on patrol over Meiktila airfield with a second FB VI – Its crew, Flt Lt C R Goodwin and Flg Off S Potts, were killed when the aircraft crashed north of Thedaw.

31
FB VI RF668/OB-J of No 45 Sqn, flown by Flg Offs Frank Scholfield, RCAF, and Reg 'Taffy' F Fussell, Jaori, June 1945
Assigned to No 45 Sqn at Cholavaram, Madras, India, on 1 April 1945, this Mosquito was one of 16 FB VIs which operated on 'cab rank' patrols from Jaori, in the Arakan, in May 1945 during Operation *Dracula* – the assault on Rangoon. Scholfield and Fussell completed their first operation in this aircraft on 13 June 1945. Painted silver overall, RF668 has had the inboard upper surfaces of its engine cowlings painted black in order to reduce glare. This aircraft was badly damaged on 26 July 1945 when Flt Lt J H Robertson got its tail up too high during a formation take-off from Cholavaram and its propellers stuck in the ground – RF668 was eventually scrapped on 8 October 1946.

FIGURE PLATES

1
Wg Cdr Hughie Edwards VC, DSO, DFC, OC No 105 Sqn at Marham in December 1942. He is wearing standard RAF officer's Battle Dress over a white turtle-necked sweater. He has a C Type flying helmet, a Type G mask, US B-7 goggles and a Mark I life jacket. Edwards has lightweight gloves on his hands and is wearing 1939 Pattern issue boots.

2
Grp Capt Max Aitken DSO, DFC, OC Banff Strike Wing at Banff in October 1944. Wearing Battle Dress 'tailor-made' of superfine material, Aitken has swapped his C Type helmet for a service dress cap. His remaining equipment is similar in style to that worn by Edwards, except for his oval-shaped goggles and steel-tipped shoes.

3
Wg Cdr John de Lacy Wooldridge DSO, DFC, DFM, OC No 105 Sqn at Marham in June 1943. Again attired in regulation Battle Dress, Wooldridge is wearing a very battered service dress cap, which was obviously an old favourite from previous tours with Bomber Command.

4
Flt Lt R W 'Sammy' Sampson, RAAF, of No 464 Sqn, RAAF, at Hunsdon in February 1944. Standing out in his matching RAAF dark blue service dress cap and Battle Dress (to which he has had an 'Australia' flash sewn onto the shoulder), Sampson is seen holding his 'Chest' type parachute, the harness for which is worn over his life jacket. His goggles, helmet, oxygen mask and gloves are all standard 1943 issue, as are his boots.

5
Wt Off Davison of No 84 Sqn, Kumbhirgam, Assam, in July 1944. He is wearing a khaki overall, a 'bush hat' with RAF puggaree flash and 'ammunition' boots. A 'Chest' type parachute harness is also worn. A standard issue webbing belt, complete with a pouch, pistol case and .38 cal service revolver, complete his equipment

6
Grp Capt Percy C Pickard DSO, DFC, attached to No 487 Sqn, RNZAF, at Hunsdon in February 1944. He is seen here moments before he climbed aboard HX922 and set off on the Amiens raid – a mission from which he never returned. Pickard is wearing an Airborne Forces 'Denison' smock over his Battle Dress, whilst a scarf, life jacket, 1938 Pattern boots and pipe complete his uniform.